2001

Look - Live & Love
Fearlessly !

Jeff

Cooking Fearlessly

Recipes and Other Adventures from Hudson's on the Bend

BY JEFF BLANK AND JAY MOORE
WITH DEBORAH HARTER
PHOTOGRAPHS BY LAURIE SMITH

ACKNOWLEDGEMENTS

Bobby Arnold, *Gastromusicologist*
Bill and Dr. Bob
Ron Brannon
Sara Courington
Kitty Crider
Mary Kilmartin
Matt Wilson
Becky Barsch Fisher, *Earl the Girl*
Abel Garcia
Adie Gonzales
Blas Gonzales
John Harms
Collin Nelson, *Straight Arrow*
Eddie Z. Safady
John Siebels
Courtney Swenson
Joan Zuckerman

CREDITS

Book Design: Pun Nio
Photography: Laurie Smith
Chef Paintings: Shanny Lott, photographed by Andrew Yates
Editing: Leta Burns, Sandy Furlong, and Bethany Powell

Produced in Association with Half Moon Bay Group

ISBN 0-9672323-0-9

Manufactured in the United States of America

Dedication

To Hudson's Staff
Past, Present and Future

For Shanny, without her, none of this
would have happened.
Thank you to our children—Ryan, Dinah, Andrew and Kristen

—Jeff Blank

For my wife Kristi Moore and our sons J.D.
and Jakob;
my parents Dan and Janie Moore and my
late great uncle, Steven Castlebury.

—Jay Moore

My friends laughed when they heard I was writing a cookbook. While no one has ever starved to death around me, my food preparation is usually more a process of opening packages, bursts of microwave rays, and ordering out. And then I met Jeff and Jay. You hang around these guys long enough, you really do believe you can cook, too. Shanny's artistic contributions went far beyond the paintings. *You* can see it in the place settings and backgrounds for the photos. We could *feel* it every step of the way. All in all, it was my fantasy come true of the way a creative collaboration can work. A lot of love and laughter went into this book, and is the unspoken ingredient in each of these recipes.

—DDH

Foreword

Okay. Or, as we Texans like to say, *awright*. I'm prejudiced. Hudson's on the Bend is one of the world's best restaurants.

Jeff Blank and Shanny Lott make it so. They do it by cooking fearlessly.

As with any restaurant, you must start with the food. And they do. These guys could cook a horseshoe and make it delicious. Instead, they specialize in dishes such as Hot 'n Crunchy Trout (my own all-time, all-world favorite) and Corn Pudding.

Downing just those two dishes and knocking them back with Ancho Bock Beer Smashers is about as close to heaven as this old wreck of a one-time oil field hand expects to get.

But their ever-changing, brave menu regularly lists dozen of good eats that are in the same league. Buffalo, antelope, armadillo—hell, even rattlesnake—they cook 'em better than anyone ever has.

You think I'm kidding about the rattlesnake? Try me. That is, try their rattlesnake sometime. They may be the only people on this or any other planet who make it taste like chicken.

This, I know, puts some folks off. But it shouldn't. You don't have to eat any such exotic dishes to love Hudson's.

For example, one member of my close family was so appalled as a child when her uncle tried to teach her to dress a deer that she became a vegetarian for life. (Keep in mind that Texan vegetarians are as rare as Valley ocelots). But she loves Hudson's. Swears their vegetarian plate is better than anything you'll find in India or Haight-Ashbury.

At the other end of the spectrum, one of my genuine cowboy friends who would be dragged behind a horse before he would eat rattlesnake or a vegetarian plate, also loves Hudson's. He swears their strip sirloin and French fries are better than buttermilk biscuits (which Jeff and Shanny can also do for you).

Besides the food, there's the service. Under general manager John Siebels' direction, the staff is friendly, courteous and fast. Siebels doubles as wine steward, good enough to shame the French according to my wife. (She's the wine expert. Longneck beer is my own specialty.)

Then there's the atmosphere, the ambiance of the place. Pure Texas. The setting is an old Lonestar limestone ranch house with a history dating back to Comanche times, situated under squat oaks on a bend in the river that catches breezes off Lake Travis.

I like to ease into the place and dinner by first having a drink on the patio. Sun tea or Wild Turkey, depending on how the week has gone. Then, move inside to a table in front of the main fireplace. (A fire is rarely needed, except when a norther rips through, but they sometimes burn some mesquite anyway, just to brighten up the room.) Have John decant a cabernet for the Mrs. and our friends. Sip awhile, then order. And afterwards, sometime long about the shank of the evening if the weather is good, move back outside for dessert and coffee under the stars. There's a nice gazebo in which to do this. Still later, if anyone has a hankering to top off the evening with a cigar and, say, a dollop of Southern Comfort, there are some far benches just right for that.

You can glide into the magic time of the first minutes after midnight, as you watch the moon rise and listen to the cottonwoods murmur.

This is the spirit and the place that gave birth to Fearless Cooking. Enjoy. And if you can't get to Hudson's, just cook up some of the stuff in this book and dream.

—Dan Rather

A Feast of Color

I remember my first box of crayons. I opened the box and saw all of those perfect points of color and smelled that waxy smell and thought, "God, I wish I could eat all of these crayons!" I really understand why children do that. It makes perfect sense to me. That was the first time I made the connection between art and food. Art is food, food is art.

The next time I made that connection was when I married Jeff Blank.

My great fortune is living with this highly creative man. He loves my work so much that Hudson's on the Bend has become my gallery, and the patrons of Hudson's have also become the patrons of my work.

What Jeff and I have discovered over the years is that bright, colorful, fearless art makes people hungry. We also learned that fearless food seems to give people the courage to buy art. We have achieved a rare and wonderful win-win situation. His work inspires my work, which in turn inspires his work. Yes, it is possible.

My paintings now hang in the homes of friends, family and strangers. They have been shipped all over the country from Boulder City, Nevada to Malibu, California and Destin, Florida. The greatest joy for me is to get to meet the people who buy my work. It is such fun to discover what connections we have and we always do.

Art is food, food is art.

Fearless Chefs

This series of paintings was inspired by a request from Jeff to paint a chef to hang in the restaurant. It spawned a whole cast of **Fearless Chefs**, one of whom is featured at the opening of each chapter. Each painting, in its own way, demonstrates the intriguing and perilous tension between the chef and his raw ingredients. Chefs have an all consuming love of food and all food gets consumed. So all things edible are doomed by this love. How tragically romantic.

The Joy of Cooking, Bossy, A False Sense of Security, A White Chef's Coat with a Pink Crustacean, Cocky, Sousey, Yam Chop, and *Maria Dulcita* were all inspired by chefs and sous chefs I have met. Confident, cocky, bossy, outrageous, gifted, energetic, joyful—they represent the ingredients that go into making a fearless chef.

Appetizers
Joy of Cooking

Here is a woman who confidently displays her talent. Her pet, the Green Breasted Foodie, is a rare and highly coveted animal who worships at the feet of all great chefs.

Salads *Bossy*

All good chefs are "Bossy." The bovine calmly grazes amongst the salad ingredients, blithely ignoring the fact that this Chef will milk her for all she's worth. This offering of radishes is just a ploy to give an internal boost to the inevitable horseradish sauce.

Soups *A False Sense of Security*

The first in the series, this painting shows a subtle portrayal of the tension between raw ingredients and chef. In this painting the plump blue birds, who have been fed well by the chef, are oblivious to the fact that they may soon be in the soup.

Fish *A White Chef's Coat with a Pink Crustacean*

Beyond being an homage to Jimmy Buffett, this painting points up the fact that if you taste good, you are the chef's best friend—but not for long. Friendly parrots stay off the menu by being tasteless whenever they get the chance.

Wings and Things *Cocky*

Cocky was the second painting in the series. Again there is tension between the cook and the cook-ee. Lulled into submission by a simple bouquet of flowers, the rooster becomes easy pickings for this somewhat sinister chef.

Meats *Sousey*

Sousey is every sous chef I have ever seen. Fresh out of school, full of energy and new ideas. She knows she can do it all and rides the wild ingredients right to the kitchen. Meanwhile the pig, with a smile on his face, is so unaware of his impending demise that he allows this means to his end on his back.

Vegetables *Yam Chop*

"Yam Chop" takes a much more Zen-like look at the life and death aspect of food preparation. In an almost meditative pose, he seems to honor the vegetable's relinquishing of its vital force.

Desserts *Maria Dulcita*

Anyone with a sweet tooth will question which element will win out in this struggle—the sugar or the chef. "Maria Dulcita," the Empress of Sugar, seems to have struck a balance in her culinary dance of temptations.

In this food

I see clearly

the presence of the entire universe

supporting my existence

–Vietnamese Buddhist monk Thich Nhat Nanh

Table of Contents

Appetizers
Snacks and
Light Meals

Meats
Wild and Tame

Salads
Beyond
Green

Vegetables
and Side Dishes

Soups
Hot and Cold

Desserts

**Fish and
Crustaceans**

**Things with
Wings**

An Introduction to Cooking Fearlessly

Never say never. To truly cook fearlessly, check your "nevers" at the door. If you never cooked "that" or think you would never eat "that"—now is the time to break new ground.

Cooking Fearlessly is about wild and great ingredients, demystifying professional techniques, a little chemistry, and a lot of fun. It's about throwing out the conventional wisdom concerning what you ought to eat, what tools to use, what goes with what, and even what might be edible. Who's to say what goes with rattlesnake, anyway?

Jeff Blank and Jay Moore are the owner and executive chef of Hudson's on the Bend restaurant outside of Austin. They have, over the last decade or so, developed a Hill Country cuisine featuring game and fish—with a taste as big and robust as Texas. In fact, the words robust and gusto might have been invented to describe the food they cook. This is not food for those afraid of flavor. Nor for the faint of heart.

"It is a big hearty taste," Jeff confesses. "If you're looking for something really mild, you're not going to find it here. All of our chefs and sous chefs really believe in a big, full, round flavor. Too often when Jay and I go out to eat at other restaurants, we find that there's nothing that really excites the tastebuds. It's like they were afraid to season it. Who were they going to offend? So we kind of jokingly started describing this situation as a fear of cooking. And we don't have it. After a while it became our motto,—*We cook fearlessly!*"

The **Fearless Philosophy** calls for exciting the tastebuds in every corner of the mouth—sweet, sour, spicy, salty. That's what we like to do with our cooking, get all the tastebuds activated at the same time.

The food at Hudson's has been inspired by the Mexican, German, Czech, American cowboy and Hill Country hunter influences in Central Texas, with an emphasis on smoking and grilling.

For those without ready access to rattlesnake or boar, recipes that feature exotic meats are presented with alternative ingredients. The **Fearless** techniques, recipes and sauces can equally enhance chicken, beef, or bass. Or, if you'd like to try something a little wild, see our *Resources section, page 178*. Many things are available by mail these days.

This book is dedicated to inspiring everyone, from those who have never cooked to those who are pros, to **Cook Fearlessly!** The philosophy challenges you to **Never Leave Well Enough Alone, Adapt and Conquer** and **When you find yourself getting too serious, stop and eat something**.

Cooking Fearlessly is about cookin' with a boogie back beat. The mood is upbeat and festive with recipes that beg to party and which make the chef look good as well as the food. That is why we often suggest appropriate music to cook by.

Cooking Fearlessly is about trusting your instincts, breaking the rules, using your hands, and inventing new tools. Some of the best recipes come out of mistakes or inspired substitutions.

big flavors

Layers of Flavors

First last and always, Cooking Fearlessly is about flavor, Flavor, FLAVOR! There's a reason why we each have 9,000 tastebuds in our mouths. Sweet and sour tastebuds live on the side of the tongue, salty is mostly in the front, and bitter is in the back. Our goal is to excite all your taste centers at once and to get your saliva squirting in anticipation. Our secret is to find ways to intensify flavor when most people back off. When you eat a meal at Hudson's, everything has a big taste.

hearty

One of the ways we provoke big flavors is by layering.

- **Layer 1**—the meat, fish, or poultry. Remember we want to enhance, not mask the flavor of the meat.
- **Layer 2**—the marinade or rub (dry marinade). *(See Salt and Seasoning section, page 8)*
- **Layer 3**—the smoke or grill flavor. *(See Smoking section, page 11 and In Your Face Grilling, page 10)*
- **Layer 4**—the sauce.

Sauce rules

Getting Saucy

Sauce rules. The secret to conquering sauce making is to have a basic understanding of wine cookery and stock. Cooking with wine is frequently misunderstood, and sometimes scares people—how can I put a half or a whole bottle of wine into this recipe? Won't we all get drunk? or Won't it taste too much like wine? Do this experiment. Take a glass of white wine (a chardonnay is good) and heat it in a saucepan on the stove until most of it evaporates and it is reduced down to about a tablespoon. As it bubbles the wine will turn golden brown and almost begin to caramelize. The alcohol burns off and most of the water, too. What is left has a divine, almost lemony flavor. The acidic properties of the wine sharpen the sour part of the taste. This is the basis of many a sauce—add cream and butter for a classic beurre blanc sauce. Add garlic for a smell that is an appetizer unto itself—causing the gastric juices to rev up in anticipation.

Stock is the mother of sauces. Again, the secret here is to reduce and intensify. Some people have fear of evaporation—"Oh my, I started with this much and now I have less."

Au contraire, as the French chefs say, the opposite is true— get rid of the water, it's not worth much, and what you have left is the taste. *(See Stock section, page 173)*

Eating Fearlessly

We promote eating the most flavorful food. Frequently such food contains fat, butter, and cream, things we have all been warned to be afraid of over the last decade. Many of these dishes are designed for special occasions or celebrations. Even we don't eat this way everyday.

There are some positive health notes in Fearless Cooking. For one, game meats are usually leaner than their domestic counterparts. Secondly, we don't think food tastes good with too much oil in it, so our recipes contain small amounts, mostly vegetable oils. We have also included plenty of good-tasting greens and vegetables. Our experience is that when food is full of flavor, people are actually less likely to overeat. Our psyches get hungry for taste as much, or more so, than our bodies hunger for real sustenance.

real
sustenance

Theory and Practice of Culinary Ferocity

Don't go off half cocked (half cooked) before beginning these recipes. It's always suggested that you read over the entire recipe, ingredients, and method, before either shopping or prepping. This will prepare you for the adventure, and will familiarize you with the route in which to proceed. We don't want you to begin without your mukluks or Swiss army knife.

Let's talk about "Mise en Place." Hey, what's a cookbook without a little French? The term essentially means "Everything in its place," "All your ducks in a row," "Your whatever together," etc. . . . you get the picture. At the restaurant, classes, and at home, we always have our ingredients assembled before beginning the cooking process. That way you are prepared to cook the dish with total attention to detail. (And not flipping out when the cream boils over 'cause you are in the fridge looking for Cuisinart parts.)

You'll be amazed at how quickly a new dish comes together and, if you're cooking in front of friends, how professional and organized you'll look!

By utilizing the theory and practice of "Mise en Place" you'll also be able to concentrate on specific recipe ingredients, such as looking at the structure of a chili pepper when you roast, peel, and seed it; knowing a roma tomato or a Creole tomato has more meat-to-seed ratio than a "Better Boy." It's the attention to small details that provides the joys and celebrations of cooking, and that nurtures the nutritional needs of body and soul.

That's the beauty of food and cooking—sensations for all five senses, the sense of accomplishment when you're finished, and the feeling of sharing a gift with friends that was made with the heart. The sharing of food is to nurture with nature.

Throughout this cookbook, we give what some may consider lengthy descriptions of the visual appearance and taste along with some of the food chemistry. We feel these are all important for pride in the finished product. While this book does have lots of simple recipes, it is more about the passion and joy of cooking— about food and its important part in the ritual of the celebration of living. We also feel this book is about abundance and the important part that it plays in feeding our souls and how, when we express it in our food, we bring it into our lives.

Keep Experimenting, Keep Learning

Auguste Escoffier, the father of Modern Cuisine, wrote in *On Cooking* 100 years ago:

"One can never know too much; the more one learns, the more one sees the need to learn more and that study as well as broadening the mind of the craftsman, provides an easy way of perfecting yourself in the practice of your art."

We offer so many substitutions of ingredients in our recipes—if you read them through first you'll have more fun creating while you shop.

We believe Cooking Fearlessly will not only stimulate the economy, it will enrich your knowledge of our entire world and the people in it. There is a culinary artist in us all—but you must cook fearlessly.

Adapt and Conquer

How to Use This Book

Each recipe is broken down into categories and accompaniments. The flavor note tells you what tastes to look for as you take your first bite of the completed recipe.

TOOLS: We like fancy tools as well as the next guy, but you don't need exotic knives and French pans to cook fearlessly. We use whatever does the job—from Exacto knives to duct tape. You can invest in a fancy smoker for your backyard, but we'll also show you how to smoke meat on the stove top or how to make your own smoker out of equipment at hand.

TIMING: We emphasize good planning. Many of the recipes in this book can be all, or partially, prepared in advance. Since part of enjoying a good meal is not being stressed out when the time comes, we encourage you to take advantage of the opportunity to break up the cooking tasks into relaxing and manageable chunks.

Philosophy: Attitude is a great seasoning. Along the way we will share with you some of our attitudes about food and cooking, as well as quotes from the great and obscure.

Musical Accompaniment **(Gastromusicology):** When we cook, we like to have music going in the kitchen, or at least in our heads. It adds to our enjoyment of the cooking process. So throughout the book we recommend music that suggests the feeling that we have about some of the dishes. Let all the senses get into the game.

Cooking Fearlessly is to formal cooking like boogie is to ballroom dancing. So, put your hands on your hips, and let your backbone slip and slide on over to the kitchen. You're about to **Cook Fearlessly.**

Salt and Seasoning

Anytime we say salt—this is what we mean.

Jeff—

The jury is still out. If your doctor has you on a restricted salt diet then listen to him/her. If not, listen to your own body—some people need more and can process more. I like more salt than Jay. It was most likely the way our mothers cooked that set our standards. While cooking in Mexico, they would always say, "Sal al Gusto"—salt as you like it.

Salt is important because it brings out the natural flavors in the food. So don't be afraid of it. Use it well.

Jay likes kosher salt because it does not have the additives—but more importantly because it's coarse and he can accurately feel how much is between his fingers when he is adding a pinch or more to a batch of sauce, or whatever. I like sea salt. It has a saltier taste so you get more bang for your buck.

Here's a trick Jay taught me. Using eyeball measuring, mix 5% white pepper, 5% cayenne pepper and 90% salt for an all purpose around-the-kitchen mix. When our recipes say add or adjust salt and pepper levels—use the mix. If you really need to watch your salt intake, use our Bronze Rub, in which salt is the least dominant ingredient.

> **Salt is important because it brings out the natural flavors in the food. So don't be afraid of it.**

Jay—

Including ground black pepper into the pepper part of the salt mixture would give it a fuller taste and hit different areas of the tastebuds. I don't care for the black pepper look in my soups and sauces, but add it if you like and call it your own!

Although any dish can be made without salt (except salt cod), just a bit added to finish a dish can be the missing ingredient that sharpens it up and makes the difference between an okay dish and a really great one. In cooking class, people sometimes cringe when they see how much salt we add. But when you break down the amount for 8–12 servings it really isn't all that much. Also . . . leave the shakers out of the kitchen.

> **Use measuring spoons or your fingers to add salt.**

Salt Mix

Using eyeball measuring, mix 5% white pepper, 5% cayenne pepper and 90% salt for an all purpose around-the-kitchen mix.

Smoke Rub

A little bit salty but goes great with anything smoked on the grill.

1 cup paprika
1/3 cup onion powder
1/8 teaspoon cayenne
1/2 teaspoon white pepper
2 teaspoons dark chili powder
3 tablespoons brown sugar
1/2 cup granulated garlic
1 teaspoon curry
1/2 teaspoon black pepper
1/4 cup kosher salt

Combine and use freely to coat meat.

Bronze Rub

Our favorite on many things, low salt with a little spice.

1/2 cup of toasted and ground coriander seeds
1 tablespoon ground onion, onion powder
3 tablespoons lemon pepper
1 tablespoon oregano, dried
1 teaspoon white pepper
1 teaspoon black pepper
1 teaspoon cayenne pepper
1 tablespoon salt

Mix together in a food processor and use freely.

Jerk Seasoning—
Extremely Fearless

No, jerk season is not the time of year when certain chefs get full of themselves. It's a highly potent, lip tingling rub for smoking or grilling.

1 cup sugar, granulated
3/4 cup garlic powder
4 tablespoons salt
1 tablespoon white pepper
1 teaspoon allspice
1 tablespoon dry mustard
3/4 cup onion powder
1/4 cup thyme, dried
1 tablespoon black pepper
1 tablespoon cayenne or 1 tablespoon habanero, ground
3 tablespoons curry
1/2 teaspoon clove, ground

Combine all ingredients. To use, coat meat with seasoning and smoke or grill.

In Your Face Grilling

Try this method of "face" testing as you cook your meats.

Yes, it takes a little experience, but the secret is as plain as the nose on your face. Try this method of "face" testing as you cook your meats.

With a "straight face" (no smiling or you'll be overdone), touch your cheek—that'll be "rare." The internal temperature of the steak will be between 110°–120° and have a cool red center.

Still poker faced, touch your chin. This is "medium rare" with the internal temperature at 120°–130° —and a warm red center.

Now touch the end of your nose. This will coincide with the texture of a "medium" steak, internal temperature 140°–145° with a hot pink center.

The area just above the bridge of your nose on your forehead is the tactile equivalent to a "medium-well" piece of meat—internal temperature 155°–160° with just a thin line of hot pinkness still left in the center.

The bottom of your shoe is well done. The internal temperature is 180° and there is no turning back (180°, get it?). Visually there is no pink. However, even though a piece of meat is well done there should be some juices left. Remember it's a well-done steak, not beef jerky.

We explained this system to Linda Werthheimer on National Public Radio's "All Things Considered." She later called us to say that when the interview aired she was in a cab in Washington, D.C. and when she looked over into the cab next to her she saw the passenger poking his face along with the explanation!

So we like ours between chin and nose, and don't forget to wash your face before dinner.

Grilling is one of our specialties and here's where we're going to let you in on the secret to grilling success. First of all, don't be afraid to get your hands dirty. And don't be afraid to get your face dirty.

If you visit a good restaurant with an open kitchen, you'll see that, as the cooks grill the meats, they seem to be touching them, as if to glean some information from them. In fact, that's exactly what's going on.

As meat cooks, the juices and moisture are reduced and it becomes firmer. Beginners frequently cut into a piece of meat to check the doneness. Not a good idea, since the juices that provide so much of the flavor run out into the grill instead of onto your tastebuds. Experienced cooks punch the meat with their fingers to check the temperature and to know when it's ready to eat.

In the Smokehouse

In a restaurant full of bold and unusual flavor combinations, the smoke house produces our favorite. Just like our menu, our smoking technique has evolved over the years.

In the beginning

When we first opened in 1984, we had a double oil-drum smoker. For those of you who did not grow up in Texas, this is two 55 gallon metal barrels welded together end to end, usually with re-bar legs. You start a small hardwood fire at one end and place whatever you are smoking at the other end, away from the heat. They usually have adjustable air vent holes at the fire end and an exhaust vent at the opposite end to allow the smoke to float around the food and season it before it exits. While this style works fine for most people, our day in and day out use took its toll, and in two months we had worn out the metal fire box. With the amount we needed to smoke at one time, we were constantly getting behind.

Movin' on up

So, since we just happened to have a group of stone masons from Mexico building our patios and sidewalks, we got them to build a sturdy 12' x 12' stone house with double thick limestone walls. Being a little short on cash and even shorter on time, we went with a galvanized metal roof. The only flaw in our construction was that we used wood two-by-sixes shielded with metal. We remember saying, "Don't worry, this is a smoker not a walk-in oven; it won't get hot enough to ignite those boards."

A short time later, a staff writer for the Food and Living section of the *New York Times* was in Austin visiting friends and wanted to write an article about us—our first chance at the big time. She informed us that she would only write the article if she could be present for the entire cooking process, start to finish. The catch was that she had only two hours.

Where there's smoke, there's fire

To speed up the process for her benefit, we fired up the smokehouse with much gusto. We were on schedule and had taken the smoked antelope leg to the kitchen to finish cooking when Jeff looked out over the writer's shoulder and saw the dishwasher run around the back of

the smokehouse and throw a bucket of water on the flaming roof. He was soon joined by other members of the kitchen staff, while Jeff and Jay tried to act like nothing was wrong and to keep the writer from looking out the window. The dish was smoked and cooked in a timely manner, the article was a huge success, and the smokehouse got a renovation.

Into the woods

We use a variety of woods for smoking. Our only rule—no telephone poles or pine trees, though we have stretched the category on occasion and had wonderful results with red aromatic cedar. We suggest starting with trees native to your "neck of the woods." We have been known to visit exotic wood shops contemplating woods from around the world. Why not? Exotic meats, exotic woods—what could be more fearless? At the other end of the spectrum, cedar shavings from the pet store work great for smoking salmon. Just get to the shavings before your kid's pet hamster.

Other tested favorites include pecan wood or pecan shells, our everyday smoking staple at the restaurant. We like the round, smooth smoke flavor of pecan and its sisters, oak and hickory. Alder is fine, too, as are the fruit woods—apple, cherry, and peach. Mesquite is okay to grill with, but we find it too strong to smoke with because of the high level of creosote. Oops, we just pissed off a couple of old Texas barbecuers.

The secret smoke of plants

We have also experimented with other kinds of plant life: dried basil stems from the herb garden, Orange Pekoe tea (great for Christmas goose or duck), and rosemary for lamb leg or loins—a strong but good flavor. For something more subtle, we sometimes put a cast iron pot with leftover wine, or beer, to simmer next to the fire, letting the flavored vapors waft onto meat or seafood.

This would not sit well with hardcore barbecue pit masters, but remember that they are usually starting with tough meat that needs to be cooked very slowly for a long time to tenderize and flavor it. We start with the best, most tender pieces of meat or seafood and add a light layer of smoke.

Smoke and Seasoning

We use smoke as a seasoning, just as we would salt, pepper, and herbs. It layers another level of flavor onto the food. It also activates a set of often neglected tastebuds in the back of the mouth—the bitter tastebuds. Smoke has a pleasing, palatable way of sneaking up on those bitter tastebuds and making them go "wow!" Grilling food does this, too, but not with the subtlety and gentleness of the smoke.

Our smoking is done for just a short time and we are working to enhance, not mask, the food's flavor. A benefit for you, as the cook, is that this kind of smoking can be done early in the day and finished inside in a standard oven just before serving. No last minute running out to the yard to see if the meat is done.

For example, for our smoked shrimp quesadilla, we smoke the shrimp for 20–30 minutes at 180°. They are not cooked all the way through. We bring them inside, refrigerate them, and finish the cooking when they go into the quesadilla. With this light smoking treatment you get juicier, moister shrimp.

Similarly with quail, we smoke to a rare to medium-rare temperature, remove them from the smoker, refrigerate, and then finish the cooking in the oven just before service.

Barrel smokers, fancy pits, stacked water smokers—there are a vast array to choose from. Here in Texas we have seen smokers made from mailboxes, old refrigerators, and huge propane tanks. Jeff has one in the chimney of his kitchen fireplace. For our style of smoking they will all work. Keep your fire low (200–220°).

Smoking Seafood

We always treat seafood differently than beef, poultry, or game, however. Because all seafood dries out quickly in the smoker, we mix 1 tablespoon of Smoke Rub with 1 cup sour cream (or yogurt) and then coat each piece of seafood (shrimp, scallop, lobster, or fish) with this mixture. The sour cream provides moisture retention and smoke attraction.

To the stove top

Our new favorite is the stove-top smoker.* It is remarkably compact and convenient. With very little prep time, on an electric or gas cooktop with no vent, you have a simple, weatherproof way to season with smoke and you won't even turn on the smoke detector.

Using one of these we have smoked a 7-oz. salmon to perfection (with just a little Bronze Rub) in 7–8 minutes.

To smoke or not to smoke? No question. Give it a try.

See Resources section.

Peppers– How to Roast
and Why We Love Them

For a mild-mannered method, you can roast them in a 450° oven (8-10 minutes) until the skin blisters. Next, remove the peppers and place them in a paper bag or airtight container (like a bowl with plastic wrap on top). This will release the skin from the chili pepper meat. Remove from the container after ten minutes and the skin will easily peel off.

If you're feeling a little bit more adventurous and active, you can also use a gas cook top or a broiler (gas or electric) to blister the skin off. But what we like to do—because it's fun and makes a good show—is to run out to the garage and dig out the propane torch. It will blister the skin off a pepper in seconds—so quickly the skin literally jumps off.

Alternately, the gourmet shops are selling fancy, cute propane torches for caramelizing sugar on crème brûlée and they will work just fine for peppers. But we prefer the higher BTU-output of the hardware store variety. Besides it being a more fearless toy—there are several culinary advantages. It burns the skin off so quickly that the pepper body does not soften or cook, and because of this, has a fresher flavor and color, as well as firmer pepper meat, which will be less likely to rip or tear when stuffing or dicing.

After removing the skin by rubbing with a dry kitchen towel, cut open and remove the seeds, seed pod, and ribs. Remember, spicy chili peppers get their heat from a chemical called capsacin. You can find most of the heat in the seeds and white ribs that run the length of the

All fresh chili peppers have an outer skin that, if removed, makes the pepper more palatable. There is more than one way to skin a pepper.

pepper. So don't rub your eye after cleaning or you'll experience the thrill of police pepper spray! Don't touch any other body parts with those hands, either. We have some funny stories we can't tell about that.

Chilies also work as an anti-depressant—no joke. When a very hot chili (jalapeño, serrano, or habanero) is munched upon, your mouth turns into a 4 alarm fire rather quickly. The brain and all of its chemicals (seratonin, endorphins, and dopamine, etc.) get activated and, via the bloodstream, run down to aid in fire control—only to find out it's just a pepper. Sure you have a hot mouth, but you also have a great natural high—and voilà—you're not depressed anymore!

Put down your Prozac and pop a pepper. If you are bi-polar you might want to have an ice cream bar for balance.

In this book we most often use five kinds of peppers

- **The Poblano** is green but sometimes has a hint of orange in it. We use this pepper the most because of its intense flavor, yet it has only a medium heat, so it is not overpowering.

- **Hatch chilies** from New Mexico are green, earthy, and mild.

- **Jalapeños** are green chilies that have their own unique flavor and are about a 6–7 on the heat scale.

- **Ancho chilies** are poblanos that have been left on the vine to turn red, and then are dried.

- **Chipotles** are smoked jalapeños. Smoking and drying reduce their heat.

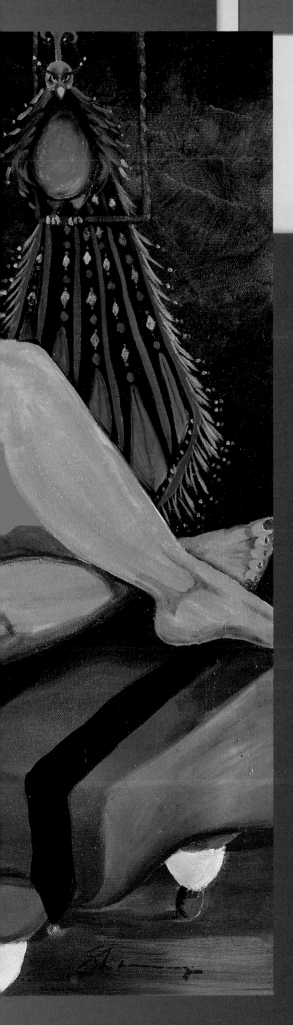

APPETIZERS,
SNACKS OR
LIGHT MEALS

Rattlesnake Cakes in a Pistachio Nut Crust with Spicy Chipotle Sauce

Smoked Shrimp Quesadillas with Peppered Jack Cheese and Flying Avocado Slices

Wild Game Enchiladas with a Chocolate Almond Mole Sauce

Texas Bandera Smoked Quail Egg Roll with New Mexico Green Pepper with Manchurian Tomatillo-Hoisin Sauce

Secret Pirated New Orleans BBQ Shrimp

Coca-Cola® Baby Back Ribs with Orange Ginger BBQ Sauce

Bock Beer Marinated Portobello Mushrooms Topped with Goat Cheese Sauce

Maine-ly Shrimp Fritters with Green Chili Lime Tartar Sauce

Succumb to the sauce and worry about laundry later.

Rattlesnake Cakes
in a Pistachio Nut Crust

with Spicy Chipotle Sauce
Serves 6–8 (2 cakes each)

Wait—don't turn the page! The Comanche Indians who once lived in the Texas Hill country believed that warriors derive great strength from eating rattlesnake. In Mexico, snake is considered an enhancer to long life. Along Highway 57, just before Matehuala, you will often find dried rattlesnake-on-a-stick for sale.

Philosophy: Never say never.

"Rattlesnake Shakes" by Omar and the Howlers, a fine Texas blues band. This is the song that was playing on the radio when this dish was first created.

Our regular customers love to bring their New York or L.A. business associates out for a little down-home snake. You too may have a business associate who deserves this memorable taste treat. It will certainly make your reputation as a fearless chef.

We originally put this on the menu with tongues firmly in cheek, but to our amazement people loved it. It has since become one of our most famous menu items and captured first place at the '94 Texas Wine and Food Festival. Check our Resources section for how to get rattlesnake by mail if you don't have some readily available.

While we encourage you to be experiment with alternate ingredients, in this case we do not recommend copperheads—too small, or water moccasins—too muddy tasting. However, iguana might do in a pinch.

VARIATIONS: If you have a rule at your house against eating reptiles, try fresh crab. We've even used chicken and pheasant (lightly sautéed or baked).

So, use your imagination and any local critters that you think appropriate. The neighbor's Doberman may be hard to catch and require a different sauce.

TIMING: Cakes can be made a day ahead, breaded, and stored in the refrigerator. Sauce can also be made ahead of time.

TOOLS:
Stock Pot or Dutch Oven
Mixing Bowl
Food Processor
Blender
Sauté Pan
Saucepan
Optional: Golf Ball

Preparing the Snake:

Combine in a 5 quart Dutch oven: 3 quarts water, 1 cup white wine, 1 yellow onion quartered, juice from 4 lemons, 2 tablespoons Tabasco®, 4 cloves of garlic, and 2 tablespoons salt (*aka* court bouillon). Submerge snake and boil the hell out of it.

Check snake after 30 minutes for doneness, adding more water as necessary. When done, remove from cooking liquid and cool slightly. Discard liquid and pull meat from bones.

The easiest meats to retrieve from the snake will be the "backstraps" from each side of the spine, with the balance coming from between the ribs. A fork will get at those hard to reach places.

Rough cut by hand until an even crab-like consistency is achieved.

Spicy "snake cake" wrapped in the caramelized nuttiness of a pistachio crust atop the smoky-creaminess of the sauce.

Rattlesnake Cakes

1 lb. rattlesnake, poached and pulled off bones
3/4 cup celery, diced
1 tablespoon garlic, minced
1/2 cup mayonnaise
2 egg yolks, beaten
2 tablespoons Creole/spicy mustard
2 tablespoons cilantro leaves, chopped
1 tablespoon basil, chopped
2 jalapenos, seeded and minced
1/4 cup bread crumbs
1 tablespoon salt

Combine all above ingredients in a large mixing bowl and blend well.

Nut Crust Mix

1 cup pistachio nuts
1/2 cup bread crumbs
Salt and pepper
1/3 cup olive oil
Chipotle Sauce

1. Chop pistachio nuts, bread crumbs, and salt and pepper to a coarse grind in a food processor.
2. With a #70 scoop or your hand, form a ball of the rattlesnake mix about the size of a golf ball or a little larger and drop into the nut crust mix. This should flatten into a 2" diameter patty. Make sure you press nut crust all around the cake.
3. Heat oil in a large sauté pan over medium-high heat to about 325–350°. At 325°, oil should shimmer like the heat coming off a hot asphalt road in summertime.
4. Sauté about 2 minutes each side until golden brown.
5. Remove from pan. Pat off excess oil and serve atop chipotle sauce.

Chipotle Sauce

2 cups good, rich chicken stock
3 cloves shallots, minced
2 large chipotle peppers
4 dashes Tabasco®
3 cloves garlic, minced
1/4 cup sundried tomatoes
1 tablespoon Worcestershire sauce
1/4 cup brown sugar, packed
2 teaspoons salt
1/2 cup cream
1 bunch cilantro (leaves only)

1. Put stock in large saucepan. Add shallots, peppers, Tabasco®, garlic, tomatoes, Worcestershire sauce, and brown sugar and simmer for 15 minutes.
2. Purée in a food processor.
3. Add salt.
4. Add cream and cilantro. Mix well.
5. Return to the pot to heat through. When reheating, bring the sauce up to a simmer and serve.

Smoked Shrimp Quesadillas

with Peppered Jack Cheese and Flying Avocado Slices

Serves 4

Never leave well enough alone. Change three ingredients and it becomes your recipe.

This is basically a Northern Mexican or Tex-Mex grilled cheese sandwich. We took the homemade Mexican white cheese quesadilla—just cheese and a flour tortilla grilled until warm—substituted peppered Jack and goat cheeses and added smoked shrimp. Voilà, a classic comfort food gets a fearless flavor boost and is transformed into a fine example of high-end Tex-Mex fusion cuisine. This is great as a passed hors d'oeuvre at a party or served with a crisp garden salad for a tasty light dinner or lunch entree. We like it best as finger food.

We will always remember this dish as the one we chose to prepare when the BBC came to film for the series "Floyd's American Pie" in our kitchen. Though scheduled for three o'clock, by the time the crew actually arrived and set-up we were well into the Saturday night dinner rush—a time when we can expect to turn out 200 meals in the space of a few hours.

Speaking of space, Hudson's on the Bend was originally a small house and the kitchen its former carport—measuring about 900 square feet. Picture six of us working in there as sort of a gridiron ballet in a subway car. Then add another six people serving. On a good night it's like a finely oiled machine, at other times the Marx Brothers would feel right at home. Now imagine six more people with cameras and lights.

Things were going as smoothly as could be expected until Jeff thwacked his knife into the pit of the avocado. Flipping it out with a flourish, he sent a succulent green piece of shrapnel into one of the 1000-watt lights, causing it to explode. Ah, show business.

VARIATIONS:
Other cheeses such as a smoked gouda or mozzarella. Instead of shrimp—strips of smoked chicken. Instead of avocado—try slices of tomato or roasted chili peppers.

TIMING:
Quesadillas can be made a day ahead. Layer between kitchen wrap or wax paper and refrigerate. Shrimp can be smoked a day ahead, cooled, and refrigerated. Note: avocados must be prepared at the last minute to preserve color and texture.

Los Aztecas Border music—aka German polka with stolen instruments.

TOOLS:
| Mixing Bowl | Rubber Spatula for Spreading Cheese |
| Sauté Pan | Turning Spatula |

A wonderful range of flavors—creamy goat cheese, rich avocado, smoky briny shrimp, and crisp browned flour tortillas.

Quesadillas

4 flour tortillas
1 avocado quartered and sliced
   lengthwise
12 each 21–25 shrimp, smoked*
   (in restaurant lingo "21–25"
   shrimp refers to 21–25 per lb.,
   larger shrimp are U-tens, under
   ten count per lb.)
1 4-oz. log goat cheese
1/4 cup grated Jack cheese
1 tablespoon garlic, minced
2 tablespoons sour cream
1/4 teaspoon each dried herbs—
   basil, oregano, thyme, and
   tarragon
2 tablespoons olive oil
1 teaspoon salt

1. Combine goat cheese, grated
   Jack, garlic, sour cream, and
   herbs in a stainless steel
   bowl.
2. Place bowl over simmering
   water. Heat to release herb
   flavors and stir together until
   smooth.
3. Remove from heat and
   slather generously over each
   tortilla.
4. Lay 3 slices of avocado over
   top 1/2 of slathered tortilla
   and place warmed, smoked
   shrimp between each slice.
5. Heat olive oil in a large sauté
   pan (non-stick surface works
   great) over medium heat.
   When hot, the oil will begin
   to shimmer—or throw in any
   leafy vegetable or a blade of
   grass for that matter and it
   will sizzle and crackle.
6. Add quesadillas and cook
   two minutes until browned.
7. Flip and cook an additional
   two minutes.
8. Cut each quesadilla into
   thirds and serve immediately.

*See Smoking section.

Wild Game Enchiladas

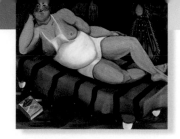

with a Chocolate Almond Mole Sauce
Serves 8. Two enchiladas per person make a hearty appetizer or light meal.

Mole (mo-lay) to a Mexican is like a bowl of chili to a Texan or a bowl of gumbo to a Cajun, or for that matter turkey stuffing to a New Englander. Each knows that *his* family recipe is the best. The actual meaning of the word "mole" is a little unclear. Some say it means "sauce," others that it means "mashed" referring to what you do to most of the ingredients. One enthusiastic eater swears that it means "Mucho Ole!"—now that's a definition hard to argue with.

This chocolate almond mole is a wonderfully rich blend of ingredients. For years moles were reserved for special occasions—fiestas—probably because of the time involved and the lengthy shopping list—but it's a great way to stimulate your taste buds and the economy—some people even claim that mole is an aphrodisiac.

Note to Hunters: This is a good recipe for the less desirable cuts from your hunting prize, such as front shoulder from venison, wild boar, elk, or anything too tough to chew without grinding up. The only requirement is that you take the time to clean the meat free of connective tissue—tedious but necessary. Remember all red meat is color coded—save the red/discard the white.

Balance heat with sweet.

"Wild Thing—you make my heart sing . . . —The Trogs"

TOOLS:
Baking Pan or Cookie Sheet
Tongs
Paper Towels
Large Saucepan
Skillet
Bowl
Knife
Food Processor with S-Blade
Cheese Grater
Spice Grinder

TIMING: The mole sauce will store safely in your refrigerator for two weeks. Freezing is okay if you must. It also makes a wonderful sauce to top grilled chicken or pork.

Wild Game Enchiladas

1 lb. wild game or beef and pork mix (can be game birds or even chicken), or any combination of the above.
1 large yellow onion, minced
3 ribs celery, minced
1 large carrot, minced
6 cloves garlic, minced
1–2 jalapeños, minced—if you want it extra spicy leave the seeds and ribs in
1 tablespoon salt, or more
2 tablespoons dark chili powder
2 tablespoons ground cumin
16 corn tortillas
3/4 lb. of Monterey Jack cheese, grated
1 cup peanut or canola oil

The Filling

1. Mince onion, carrots, garlic, and jalapeño in a processor with an S-blade. The food processor bowl should be about 1/2 full, which is why we always buy the one with the biggest food bowl. Rough chop veggies first; make sure you have a sharp blade. Never overload your food processor.
2. Hand chop the celery because it gets stringy if chopped in the processor.
3. Grind or mince the meat with a sharp knife or food processor S-blade.
4. Pre-heat a large skillet or saucepan over medium-high heat.
5. Brown meat until most of the fat is rendered off.
6. Add veggies and spices.
7. Simmer 20 minutes and set aside to cool.

The Tortillas

1. In a large skillet, heat peanut or canola oil over medium-high heat until it shimmers—325–350° fry

temperature. It's good to have paper towels handy to suck up extra oil.

2. Using tongs, dip the corn tortillas in the hot oil for 3–4 seconds each and lay them out on the paper towels to drain. If you were in Mexico these would be fried in animal fat—tasty si, healthy no.

3. Lay out tortillas on the countertop and put about 1 oz. of meat and 1/2 oz. of cheese on each.

4. Roll them up. Rolling works best while they are still warm from the oil bath.

5. Place them in a baking pan or casserole, top with sauce, and heat in a 350° oven for 15 minutes.

6. Sprinkle with cheese and heat 2 more minutes, then serve.

The Sauce

1 cup celery
1/2 cup carrot
1/2 cup yellow onion
6 cloves garlic
2 jalapeños, seeds and all
1/2 cup olive oil
2 tablespoons Mexican oregano (regular will work)
1/2 cup chili powder
1/2 cup ancho chili, puréed (rehydrate in water/spin down in blender)
1/2 cup tomato paste
1/4 cup cumin
1 cup almonds, sliced
1/2 cup sesame seeds
5 cups good chicken stock
1/2 cup Worcestershire sauce
1/2 cup brown sugar
8 oz. dark semi-sweet chocolate
2 bunches cilantro—leaves only, chopped
2 teaspoons salt, or to taste

1. Toast 1/2 cup sesame seeds in a dry skillet until lightly browned. Set aside to cool. Toast almonds the same way. Grind separately in spice grinder.

2. Mince celery finely by hand before adding to carrots, onions, garlic, and jalapeño in the food processor. Purée until all are mashed together.

3. Sauté veggies in very hot olive oil until caramelization just begins.

4. Add oregano, chili powder, ancho pepper, tomato paste, cumin, almonds, sesame seeds and sauté 8–10 minutes.

5. In a large saucepan, bring chicken stock, Worcestershire sauce, and brown sugar to a boil.

6. Add sautéed ingredients and simmer for 10 minutes.

7. Add chopped cilantro and chopped chocolate.

8. Remove from heat and stir until chocolate melts into the sauce.

9. Correct seasoning with salt.

Note: When reheating sauce, bring to a simmer (180°).

Wild, dark, rich, mysterious with all the spice and romance of old Mexico.

Texas Bandera Smoked Quail Egg Roll
with New Mexico Green Pepper
with Manchurian Tomatillo-Hoisin Sauce

Serves 6–8

To get all these flavors together we crossed county lines, state lines, and an ocean. The Bandera quail is from Bandera, Texas—as the quail flies, about an hour from the restaurant. We get our goat cheese from Dripping Springs in Hays county, and Hatch chilies from New Mexico are the best. Traditional oriental hoisin sauce takes an entirely new turn when mixed with Hudson's famous tomatillo white chocolate sauce (TWCS)—an incredibly rich green mole.

TWCS was created shortly after Jay began at Hudson's. Jeff had been waxing poetic about the wonderfully rich sauces he had tasted on a trip to the interior of Mexico. This inspired Jay to "improve" the tomatillo sauce with white chocolate (in the Moore family they say "Moore is More"), and so it was.

Wild East meets the Wild West and tastes Wild.

"Bandera"
—*Willie Nelson*

VARIATION:
6 smoked chicken thighs

TIMING:
It's a good idea to smoke the bird ahead of time—a day ahead is good. You can also wrap the rolls as much as six hours ahead and refrigerate.

TOOLS:

Food Processor or Sharp Knife

Pastry Brush

Spoon

Paper Towels

Tongs

Wok or 5-qt. Dutch Oven

Texas Bandera Smoked Quail

6 boneless smoked quail, small dice
1/4 cup Bronze Rub
1/2 cup diced green chilies, Hatch or Anaheims
1/2 cup goat cheese
1 tablespoon shallots, minced
2 tablespoons garlic, minced
1/2 cup jicama, small dice
1 bunch green onion tops, fine dice
2 bunches cilantro leaves, roughly chopped
2 limes, juiced
1 teaspoon salt
1 egg
1/2 cup milk
16 egg roll wrappers
1 quart canola or vegetable oil

1. Smoke quail using 1/2 Bronze Rub *(see Smoking section)*. Set aside.
2. Dice the smoked quail and mix with remaining Bronze Rub.
3. Combine chilies, goat cheese, shallots, and garlic and reserve.
4. Mix jicama, green onion, chopped cilantro, lime juice, and salt and reserve.
5. Whisk the egg with the milk to make egg wash.
6. In center of each egg roll wrapper, place 1 tablespoon quail mixture, 1 tablespoon goat cheese mixture, and 1 tablespoon jicama mixture.
7. Fold egg roll wrappers around fillings. Follow the directions on the package. Brush last fold with egg wash to seal.
8. Deep fry in oil until golden brown. Do this in batches of 4 so the oil doesn't cool down. The egg rolls will float, so you will have to keep turning them to get even browning. It will probably take a couple of minutes to crisp the outside and heat the innards. If rolls have been refrigerated, increase cooking time to 3–4 minutes.

Tomatillo White Chocolate Sauce*

Yield: 3 cups

1/2 cup chicken stock
1 tablespoon garlic, minced
1 tablespoon red onion, diced
2 cups tomatillos, husks removed and quartered
1 jalapeño, chopped
1/4 cup almonds
2 tablespoons sesame seeds
2 limes, juice and zest
2/3 cup white chocolate chips
1/2 tablespoon cornstarch
1 tablespoon water
1 1/2 bunches cilantro, leaves only
1/2 tablespoon salt and pepper blend

1. Separately toast almonds and sesame seeds in a dry skillet until lightly browned.
2. Purée stock, garlic, onion, tomatillos, jalapeño, almonds, sesames, lime juice, and zest in a food processor.
3. Transfer to a sauce pot, bring to a simmer over medium heat and incorporate chocolate, stirring until smooth.
4. Combine cornstarch and water until smooth and stir into sauce. Bring to a boil and remove from heat.
5. Purée cilantro in blender with 1/2 the hot sauce. Careful now!
6. Return to pot and mix together.
7. Adjust seasoning with salt and pepper blend.

Manchurian Tomatillo-Hoisin Sauce

1 cup Hudson's on the Bend Tomatillo White Chocolate Sauce*
1/2 cup rice wine vinegar
1/4 cup hoisin sauce (soybean and garlic sauce found in the oriental food section of most grocery stores)
1 tablespoon dark toasted sesame oil
1 teaspoon fish sauce (You may need to go to an oriental market for this one)
2 tablespoons lime juice

Whisk together and serve in dipping bowl, or under eggrolls.

This is our most secret recipe, so don't tell anyone. To be fair, we won't tell anyone if you use the stuff from the jar and say you made it. See Resources section for overnight delivery.

The heat, the cream, the smoke plus the crunch of the wrapper and the wang from the sauce.

Secret Pirated New Orleans BBQ Shrimp

4–5 large shrimp per person as an entrée for 4 or can be an appetizer for 8

This dish originally came to us from a restaurant in the French Quarter. As frequently happens in the food community, this "secret" recipe was just too good to resist. The truth is, stealing recipes is a favorite pastime of chefs. The story on this one is that one enterprising restauranteur purloined a sample of this sauce and had it analyzed in a lab to figure out the ingredients. A pirated version made its way to us, then we added a little Hudson's on the Bend attitude. This is one of our favorites during the summer.

This is truly an appetizer, something that excites and feeds the hunger. The sauce has a heady aroma that will fill the room and you may experience an overwhelming desire to sample as you cook. It's best to make a bit extra to nosh on or have the next course at the ready. We cook the shrimp with shells on and serve it with lots of fresh bread to sop up the juice. The larger the shrimp, the better the dish, even jumbo crayfish will work. The shrimp can be cooked without the shells to make the dining process more fastidious, however, our best advice is to roll up your shirt sleeves, eat with both hands, and throw the shrimp shells over your shoulder. Though it's best to be outside when throwing food.

Succumb to the sauce and worry about laundry later.

"Secret Agent Man" —Johnny Rivers

VARIATION: As an entrée this dish pairs nicely with rice. We also love to put our ancho bock beer smashed potatoes in the center of the plate and surround it with shrimp and sauce for the all-orange plate.

TIMING: Sauce can be made up to 3–4 days in advance and you can pull this meal together in half an hour.

TOOLS:
6–7 Quart Saucepan or Wok
Tongs
Shell Dish
Bib
Finger Bowls/Lemon Water or Garden Hose

Secret Pirated New Orleans BBQ Shrimp

Shrimp—1/4 lb. per person—2 lbs. total; we recommend 16–20 shrimp or larger
2 tablespoons red onion, minced
1 lb. butter
4 tablespoons garlic, minced
1 teaspoon salt
2 bay leaves
3/4 cup rosemary (It's got to be fresh)
1/2 teaspoon dried oregano
1/2 teaspoon dried basil
2 tablespoons paprika
2 teaspoons cracked black pepper
1/2 cup lemon juice—the juice of 6 lemons, plus zest of 3
1/2 tablespoon cayenne pepper—depending on how hot you want it

1. Simmer all ingredients except shrimp in a 6–7 quart saucepan (or the largest one you have) for 10 minutes.
2. Add shrimp and cook until pink (5 minutes) on medium-low heat.
3. Serve in a large bowl with a bib and lots of bread.

The magical combination of butter, garlic, and rosemary with the heat from the cayenne.

Coca-Cola® Baby Back Ribs

with Orange Ginger BBQ Sauce

6 people or 2–3 people per rack as an appetizer

This recipe was a gleam in Jay's eye from way back when he was a student at the CIA. That's the Culinary Institute of America in Hyde Park, New York (not that other place in Langley, Virginia). The class was divided into groups and told to plan their dream restaurant—a big-deal assignment and highly competitive. Each one tried to outdo the other in place settings and menu.

Jay's team called upon his Texahoma roots for inspiration. They competed against the white tablecloths and elegant place settings with a down-home barbecue restaurant. There were menus on the placemats, plastic squirt bottles on the tables, and the leading entree: Coca-Cola® Baby Back Ribs. A feast for the barbecue-deprived in upstate New York.

When the professors (a somewhat snooty crowd more inclined to haute cuisine) completed their judging, they had smiles on their faces and sauce under their fingernails. And guess who got the highest grade?

Coke® is said to be able to remove rust from a chrome car bumper—but the same ingredients make the ribs oh-so tender and leave a unique sweet flavor in the meat.

The universe is full of magical things patiently waiting for our wits to grow sharper.

"Boogie Back to Texas" —Asleep at the Wheel

TIMING:
Soak ribs for 24 hours.

Coca-Cola® Baby Back Ribs

1 gallon Coke® syrup; Coke® syrup is the concentrated product before the carbonated water is added. It is not usually sold direct to the public, but try your local bottler. Sometimes a favorite small restaurant with a bar will be inclined to accommodate you if you are very nice or twist the right arms.
OR
Get 2 2-liter bottles of regular Coke and reduce down to a quart of syrup by simmering over low heat.
2 Racks o'-ribs—A baby back is about 12–15 ribs, the ones we use weigh 1 3/4 lbs. or less—small—and most readily available. We like that meat-to-bone ratio.
Smoke Rub
Orange Ginger BBQ Sauce

1. Submerge ribs in coke syrup for 24 hours in a casserole dish. It's okay to cut the rack in half to fit the pan. The half racks will also fit in a large airtight bag. Add the marinade, remove the air. Get the high-security bags to avoid a real mess.
2. Remove from marinade and season with the Smoke Rub *(see Salt and Seasoning section)*.
3. Smoke 'em. Approximately 1 1/2 hours at 220° *(see Smoking section)*. When done, slice and serve atop orange Ginger BBQ Sauce.

TOOLS:
Large Casserole Dish to Marinate Ribs (or Airtight Plastic Bags)
Large Skillet for Sauce
Food Processor
Smoker

Baby back ribs are always best straight off the smoker. They are good the second reheat but are never as tender and juicy as the first bite.

Orange Ginger BBQ Sauce

This is a barbecue sauce that's not really a barbecue sauce in the traditional sense of the word—its two predominant flavors are orange and ginger. Jeff came across it while dining at a restaurant in downtown Dallas called Dakotas and decided to recreate it for Hudson's. After several failed attempts, he gave up on fresh orange juice and switched to frozen concentrate—a 4 to 1 concentration—and bingo! We are not privy to how the Minute Maids™ remove the water from fresh juice, but it's better than boiling and we thank them.

2 oz. bacon, ground in a food processor
    with S-blade before cooking
1/3 cup onion, finely diced
1 tablespoon garlic, chopped
1/2 cup ginger, chopped (It's gotta be
    fresh)
2 teaspoons black pepper
1/3 cup brown sugar
3 tablespoons Worcestershire sauce
1/3 cup orange juice concentrate
3 tablespoons champagne vinegar
1 teaspoon Tabasco®
1 3/4 cups catsup
1 teaspoon salt

1. Cook bacon.
2. Add onion, garlic, ginger and black pepper and sweat until onions are translucent.
3. Add brown sugar, Worcestershire sauce, orange juice concentrate, vinegar, and Tabasco® and bring to a boil.
4. Add catsup and simmer 10 minutes.
5. Adjust seasoning with salt and pepper.

VARIATION:
This is one of the recipes we put in a bottle, so if you want to taste before you try making it yourself, call our 800 number and we will ship it to you. (See Resources section.) It's great with grilled foods of all kinds—try summer shrimp in it or put a little on top of a grilled tuna steak.

The sweetness of coke, that tartness of citrus, the zing of ginger with the texture of tender meat sucked off the bone.

Bock Beer Marinated Portobello Mushrooms

Topped with Goat Cheese Sauce

Serves 4

We are going to assume if you have this cookbook and have read this far—you are most likely not a vegetarian. Frankly we're carnivores and have been known to say "we love animals—they're delicious". But you never know when a non-meat eater will surface, and these mushrooms are juicy and flavorful enough to please all.

The Portobellos that we use are just fully matured Crimino mushrooms. Which in turn is a variation of white button mushrooms. Yes, who would imagine that those mild-mannered mushrooms which you see in the grocery store, when left to grow outside, will turn into wild and woolly steak mushrooms. Give 'em a little beer—they're happy and so are you.

Because they are matured, the cap is open. With the gills exposed some of the moisture has escaped, which results in a more intense flavor and a dense meaty texture. We sort of picture them as biker mushrooms, though the fancy name— "Portobello" or "Portobella" was the creation of some marketing guy in the '80s trying to add panache to this diamond-in-the-rough fungus.

A romantic name, a little fungus, and a great sauce will get you far.

Fantasia Soundtrack—picture the dancing mushrooms.

VARIATION: We couldn't resist putting lightly sautéed crab meat on top.

TIMING: Marinate 24 hours in advance. Grill just before serving. Sauce can be made a day ahead of time.

TOOLS:
Marinating Casserole or Airtight Bag
Grill or Sauté Pan
Medium Saucepan
Spoon

Bock Beer Marinated Portobello Mushrooms

4 big mushroom caps or 8 small ones—stems removed
2 cans or bottles Shiner Bock or a bock beer from your area
1/2 cup brown sugar, packed
2 tablespoons garlic, finely chopped
2 tablespoons red onion, finely diced
1/4 cup Worcestershire sauce
6 shakes Tabasco®
1/4 cup lime juice
2 tablespoons Creole or whole grain mustard
1 teaspoon salt
1/4 cup olive oil
Goat Cheese Sauce

1. Combine beer, sugar, spices, and half the oil.
2. Pour over mushrooms and marinate 24 or more hours before serving. We like to marinate in an airtight plastic bag.

The velvety smooth richness of the Texas goat cheese sauce is set off by the robust sharpness of the Bock beer marinade and the earthiness of the mushroom.

3. Our favorite preparation is to grill the marinated caps over a pecan wood fire, but they can be sautéed as an alternative. Before sautéing, heat 2 tablespoons of olive oil in a sauté pan over medium-high heat.

4. Pat the mushrooms dry and sauté gill side up for two minutes. This will caramelize the tops and add flavor.

5. Turn the mushrooms after two minutes and cook an additional 1–2 minutes to heat through.

6. Remove from pan and slice at intervals with a serrated knife on a 45° angle. Transfer to a plate and top with goat cheese sauce.

Goat Cheese Sauce

1 cup chardonnay
2 tablespoons red onion, small dice
2 tablespoons garlic, minced
2 cups heavy cream
1 teaspoon each, dried basil, oregano, tarragon, and thyme
8 oz. local goat cheese
1 cup Monterey Jack cheese, shredded
1/4 cup sour cream
1 teaspoon salt

1. Combine wine, red onion, and garlic and reduce over medium-high heat until almost dry.

2. Add heavy cream.

3. Heat and reduce by 25 percent over medium heat.

4. Reduce heat to low and whip in herbs, goat cheese, Jack cheese, sour cream, and salt.

Maine-ly Shrimp Fritters

with Green Chili Lime Tartar Sauce

Makes about 16 fritters or 8 hearty appetizers.

The late esteemed culinarian, James Beard, loved clam fritters. As a salute to him, we took his favorite recipe and gave it a Gulf Coast twist—featuring the flavors of poblano pepper and cilantro. While cooking this recipe for 600 people at a benefit for the Austin Art Museum, we hit upon the idea of adding some lobster to the mix. Lo and behold, we discovered that as the crustaceans increased, so did the quality of the dish.

Topped with Green Chili Tartar Sauce—a tartar sauce that pushes the edge of the tartar sauce envelope—it becomes one of those have-to-have appetizers. This can become a lunch or light dinner by making the fritters a little bigger.

"If it ain't fried, it ain't food."
—Earl the Girl

"Don't take those boats out to sea"
—Guy Clark

VARIATIONS: Crab, lobster, catfish, oysters, and clams would also love to be "frittered." Try this on top of garden greens tossed in creamy lime basil dressing.

TIMING: Because of bubbling action from the soda and baking powder, it is best to use the batter soon after mixing. The fritters will be lighter and fluffier. The sauce can be made a day ahead of time and refrigerated.

TOOLS:
Food Processor
Bowl
Whisk
Large Skillet or Fry Pan
Spoon or Ladle
Paper Towels
Zester

Note: Some of us have been known to eat these as we're cooking them—"One for you, two for me—oops there's not enough!" Sooo, if you have a hungry kitchen helper, this only makes enough for 6. Jeff eats these without the sauce as he's cooking, so that can also muck up the proportions. As always, use your own judgment, it's your kitchen.

Maine-ly Shrimp Fritters

1 lb. shrimp, peeled
1/2 lb. lobster tail meat
1 tablespoon baking soda
2 tablespoons baking powder
1 cup all purpose flour
2 large eggs
2 limes, juice and zest
1/2 cup milk
1 tablespoon butter, melted
2 tablespoons buttermilk
1 tablespoon garlic, minced
1 poblano pepper, peeled, seeded, and
   diced 1/4" *(See Pepper section)*
Pinch of cayenne pepper
1 1/2 tablespoons salt
2 cups vegetable oil (peanut, canola)
Green Chili Lime Tartar Sauce

1. Purée shrimp and lobster in food processor.
2. Mix baking soda, baking powder, and flour in large bowl.
3. Whisk together eggs, lime juice and zest, milk, melted butter, buttermilk, garlic, poblano pepper, cayenne pepper, and salt.
4. Whisk together the results of steps 2 and 3. Fold in shrimp and lobster.
5. In a large skillet or fry pan pour oil to about 1/3" deep and heat to 350° (just before smoking over) on medium-high heat. A leaf of cilantro will crackle when dropped into oil when it is the right temperature.
6. Using a large spoon or ladle, drop about 2–3 tablespoons of batter per fritter in oil, cook until golden brown, and flip. Keep oil hot by not over-crowding. About 2–3 minutes per side.
7. Set on paper towel when golden brown and repeat.
8. Serve topped with Green Chili Lime Tartar Sauce.

Green Chili Lime Tartar Sauce

This Southwest tartar sauce is our favorite on fried seafood. Fried catfish is heaven with this on top. The secret to this recipe is finding the right kind of green chili pepper—the long New Mexico or Texas chili is the best.

A poblano pepper will work. They're a little hotter—about a 5 on a scale of 10. A

lot of good groceries and gourmet shops now carry frozen and roasted green chili peppers—which are also okay if you can't get fresh.

2 cups green chili peppers
1 red bell pepper
2 cups mayonaise
1/4 cup garlic, minced
1/4 cup capers, drained
3 bunches cilantro—leaves only
5 limes, juice and zest

1. Blister and peel skin from peppers (see Pepper section).
2. Cut peppers in half, remove the seeds and veins, and dice into 1/4" pieces. Reserve the red bell pepper and an equal part of the green chili pepper for garnish.
3. The rest of the green chili pepper goes into the food processor with all the other ingredients and is pulsed to blend.
4. Chill and serve on top of shrimp fritters with green and red chili pepper garnish.

The textures make this dish so pleasing the rich pillowy fritter with the shrimp flavor, topped with the tart powder of the green chili lime tartar sauce.

Sometimes the things that are meant to be together are hiding at the back of your refrigerator.

SALADS—
BEYOND
GREENS

Spinach Salad with Hot Honey Mustard and Bacon Dressing Topped with Smoked Quail Dipped in a Honey Cilantro Ginger Glaze

Toasted Piñon-Coriander Crusted Goat Cheese Atop Garden Greens Tossed in a Poblano-Almond-Lime Vinaigrette

Fearlessly Stalking the Late Summer Tomato—A Tasting Adventure

Iced Asparagus and Spring Berry Salad with Blood Orange Vinaigrette

Composed Fruit and Flower Salad with Guava Coconut Vinaigrette

Southwestern Caesar Salad Topped with Tabasco® Croutons and Smoked Shrimp

Garden Greens with Lime Basil Dressing Topped with Pan-Seared Scallops

Chilled Lobster and Texas Dewberry Coleslaw

Jicama and Tomatillo Salad with Gingered Lime Vinaigrette

Spinach Salad with Hot Honey Mustard and Bacon Dressing

Topped with Smoked Quail Dipped in a Honey Cilantro Ginger Glaze

Serves: 6–8

We sometimes refer to this recipe as "the salad that vegetarians fear." We'll slyly suggest that we "just have salad tonight," and by the time we're through, there's meat everywhere and grease on the greens. Ah, but it *is* the most popular salad at the restaurant. People like to order it with an appetizer for a light meal.

Spinach is grown in sandy soil, so it's best to wash it well. Pluck or pull the large stems and veins from the leaves and float the leaves in a sink or large bowl of water. Agitate, then let it rest. Gravity will finish the job. Lift the spinach from the water and drain well. Curly leaf or flat leaf varieties are both good and have loads of iron and vitamins A and C.

Go ahead and use a semi-boneless quail. They are available at better butcher shops.

Salads don't have to be light or low fat.

"Greasy Greens"
—Steve James

VARIATIONS: Squab, duck, pheasant, wood pigeon, dove or goose can all stand-in for quail and be tasty—okay, okay, chicken, too.

TIMING: You can make the dressing and glaze the day before and reheat, pulling everything together quickly.

Spinach Salad

1 smoked quail per person *(see Smoking section)*
1 handful spinach per person
Sliced mushrooms, julienned green apples, and red onions for
  garnish

Hot Honey Mustard and Bacon Dressing

1 cup Creole mustard or coarse-grained tarragon mustard
1/2 cup Hudson's champagne herb vinegar
1/2 cup honey
1 cup bacon, diced into bits

1. Cook the bacon in a single layer, drain and crumble.
2. Mix the bacon, vinegar, 1/2 cup honey and mustard together in a saucepan and bring to a light simmer.

TOOLS:
Smoker
Pastry Brush
Sauce Pot
Whisk
Bowl
Sauté Pan

Honey Cilantro Ginger Glaze

1 1/2 cups honey
1/4 cup soy sauce
1/4 cup Worcestershire sauce
1/3 cup fresh ginger, minced
1/4 cup garlic, minced
1/4 cup shallots, minced
2 bunches cilantro, leaves only
Salt and pepper to taste, 1 teaspoon minimum
1/4 lb. sweet butter

1. Combine all glaze ingredients in a saucepan and bring to a simmer over medium heat; simmer for 4 minutes. Hold on warm, at 180° or less.
2. Smoke quail *(see Smoking section)*. This can be done earlier in the day. Re-warm quail in a 250° oven for 5 minutes after dipping it in the glaze.
3. To assemble salad, toss hot dressing onto cold spinach, 1/4 cup per salad.
4. Garnish with sliced mushrooms, julienned apples, and red onions.
5. Dip quail in glaze one more time. Rest quail, glazed and hot, atop the wilted spinach salad.

Smoky quail dipped in sweet honey glaze with the surprise of ginger atop wilted greens coated with the richness of bacon and mustard.

Toasted Piñon-Coriander Crusted Goat Cheese

Atop Garden Greens Tossed in a Poblano-Almond-Lime Vinaigrette

Serves 4

This dish has evolved fearlessly over the years. It started out as an oriental recipe featuring a pattern of black and white sesame seeds, which eventually transmogrified into almonds and sesames with a stop along the way at pumpkin and sesame. "Won't stick to most dental work," notes Jay, which he is inclined to say because his father is a dentist. Dr. Moore used to give out toothbrushes at Halloween, to Jay's eternal embarrassment.

This salad is a marvelous marriage of texture and flavors. Some people are put off by goat cheese because they associate it with a strong smell. Perhaps they have had the more odiferous French Montrachet or Mexican goat cheese, sold by the side of the road wrapped in pantyhose instead of cheesecloth. But Larson Farm, our supplier in Dripping Springs, produces a mildly flavored cheese that's not dry or chalky. The secret is that they keep the Billies away from the Nannies when they're producing milk.

We enhance the creamy richness of the cheese with a crust of buttery, toasted pine nuts, and tart, crunchy coriander. Assemble this as a treat for yourself and enjoy the sensations. Be careful not to over process the pine nuts. They have a tremendous amount of oil and will easily become "Coriander Flavored Pine Nut Butter."

Opposites attract—and they meet in poetic splendor—then disappear.

"I've got the toasted-piñon-coriander-crusted-goat-cheese-atop-garden-greens-tossed-in a Poblano-Almond-Lime-Vinaigrette Blues"
—sung by you with lots of angst

VARIATIONS: Use any nuts you want—almonds to macadamia, whatever nuts live in your neighborhood. In the dressing, substitute bell pepper for a milder taste if you prefer.

TIMING: Because it takes so little time to warm the crusted cheese for the salad, we pre-roast the nuts and coriander for optimum flavor. Dressing can be made a day ahead if needed, and goat cheese wheels can be rolled in the nuts.

TOOLS:
Blender
Food Processor
Propane Torch

Toasted Piñon-Coriander Crusted Goat Cheese atop Garden Greens

3/4 cup pine nuts
1/2 cup coriander seeds
1 goat cheese log (4–6 oz.)
3/4 teaspoon salt

1. Toast pine nuts and coriander seeds separately in a dry skillet, stirring all the time until lightly toasted. Set aside to cool slightly before processing.
2. Combine pine nuts, coriander seeds and salt in the food processor and pulse until coarsely ground. Be careful not to over process. Remove and place on a plate.
3. Cut a 6-oz. cheese log into 4 equal wheels.
4. Press down gently to flatten. Coat all sides of the cheese wheel with the nut mixture.
5. Place on a baking sheet in a 375° oven for 5–7 minutes or until soft.
6. Serve atop dressed salad greens.

Poblano-Almond-Lime Vinaigrette

3 roasted poblanos
3/4 cup almonds, sliced
1/4 cup sesame seeds
1 cup granulated sugar
3/4 cup lime juice
1/4 cup garlic, minced
1/4 cup shallots, minced
1 1/2 cup rice wine vinegar
1 1/2 teaspoon salt

1. Blister and peel skin from poblano peppers *(see Pepper section)*.
2. Cut them in half and remove seeds and veins.
3. Toast almonds and sesame seeds separately in a dry skillet, stirring all the time until lightly browned. Cool slightly.
4. Combine all ingredients in a blender and process until smooth.

This recipe makes about a quart of vinaigrette. It lasts for weeks in the refrigerator, so save what you don't use.

The crisp coolness of the dressed greens is a wonderful frame for the cheese. The vinaigrette is a blend of poblano spiciness, toasted nut richness balanced with the tartness of limes and rice wine vinegar.

Fearlessly Stalking the Late Summer Tomato

A Tasting Adventure
Serves 6

In this recipe, the ingredients and the process are inextricably linked, so read all the way through before you go shopping. This experience can be repeated over and over again and never be the same twice.

"I have the simplest tastes. I am always satisfied with the best."
–Oscar Wilde

"There's only two things in life that money can't buy, and that's true love and home-grown tomatoes."

"Homegrown Tomatoes"
—Guy Clark

Evergreen, Golden Jubilee, Big Rainbow . . . Green Zebra, Red Currant, Cherokee Purple, Great White . . . Early Cascade, Super Sweet 100 and Nebraska Wedding—these are names of some of the heirloom tomatoes that are making a big comeback. The term "heirloom" means that they have not been hybrid or crossbred for any reason. These are old strains grown strictly for flavor. And the quest for flavor is what we're all about.

This salad provides an exploration of, and perhaps an education in, the balsamic vinegars, olive oils, cheeses and herbs that complement tomatoes. It calls for doing what we like best—going to the market with plenty of money, no list, and the knowledge that we are about to buy some things that we have never tasted before.

You may want to share this tasting experience with a guest. Sharing can frequently enhance the flavor of food when the guest is chosen selectively. True tomato-lovers proclaim its aphrodisiac-like powers, in fact the French call them pommes d'amour, "love apples" . . . and the French are rarely wrong about food or love. One of the gardening catalogs even sells a tomato-scented perfume.

VARIATION: Tomatoes always taste better if they're vine-ripened and picked from your own garden.

TIMING: It's best to do your tomato shopping two days prior to the meal so the fruit has time to ripen on your windowsill. Tomatoes that are fully ripened can go in your refrigerator to slow the ripening process.

TOOLS:
Sharp Knife and a Credit Card

Fearlessly Stalking the Late Summer Tomato

3 kinds of balsamic vinegar
3 kinds of olive oil
5 types of tomatoes
2–3 cheeses you have never tried before
Basil, Fresh!
A good bread is a must to help you cleanse the palette between mouthfuls.

1. Go the grocery store. Gather at least 3 kinds of balsamic vinegar, from moderate to expensive to very expensive. Then do the same with the olive oil. We suggest you don't buy anything cheap.

2. Gather a selection of at least 5 types of tomatoes and mark down their names, noting which are organic, hot house, whatever makes them special. This is all part of the taste education experience. You may have to go to more than one store or, better yet, a good road-side vendor, or your neighbor's garden to round out the selection.

3. Next head to the cheese section and gather 2–3 cheeses you have never tried before. Texas goat cheese from Larson Farm in Dripping Springs, buffalo mozzarella from Dallas, some different Mexican cheeses— queso fresca or whatever is local.

4. If you don't have any fresh basil growing in your garden (shame on you—it grows like a weed!), buy some fresh, if only for the pleasure of smelling it in the kitchen while you cook.

5. Now for the assembly . . . all the ingredients should be at room temperature. Arrange tomatoes and cheeses decoratively on the plate. Savor the differences in color and texture—use your imagination and eyes.

6. Garnish with chiffonade of basil. A fancy word "chiffonade," which literally translated means "made of rags." Just fold fresh large basil leaves in half length- wise and chop into thin slices. Voilà, chiffonade!

7. Serve your vinegars and oils on the side so you can taste each one separately and pick your favorite combinations of flavors.

Note: You now know how to make a fifty-dollar salad for four—just kidding. You don't have to spend anywhere near that much, but if you start buying 25-year old balsamic vinegar and twenty-dollar olive oil, it can add up. Look at it this way, it's cheaper than going to Italy and you'll have broadened your mind and your larder with enough balsamic vinegar and olive oil to make many, many salads.

Iced Asparagus and Spring Berry Salad

with Blood Orange Vinaigrette

Serves 8

While Joni Mitchell was right, "They've paved paradise and put up a parking lot," the hardy asparagus springs eternal. It has grown through several asphalt parking lots in Southern California, pushing chunks of asphalt skyward as the tender shoots reach for the sun. Those pesky developers didn't know how persistent those old asparagus fields could be.

Blood oranges are a sweet and tart fruit with red pulp. They taste like someone at the fruit factory mixed up a sweet grapefruit with an orange. In fact if you can't find blood oranges, mix 1/2 grapefruit juice with regular orange juice and the flavor will be very similar.

Iced crisp asparagus with berries—a sure sign winter is over! This salad is all the best of spring— tender greens and the juicy perfection of berries and fruits.

Asparagus—plant it properly and you have it for the rest of your life.

"It's gonna be a bright, bright sunshiny day"
"I can see clearly now"
—Jimmy Cliff

VARIATION: This dressing is wonderful with orange and grapefruit segments tossed with garden greens and topped with fresh berries.

TOOLS:
6–7 Quart Pot
Vegetable Peeler
Knife
Blender

TIMING: Dressing can be made a day or two in advance. Asparagus can be done ahead, too, as long as you keep it chilled and drained.

Iced Asparagus and Spring Berry Salad

40 pieces asparagus—5 shoots per person
Seasonal fruit: strawberries, raspberries, blackberries, kiwi or star fruit
1 tablespoon salt
1 tablespoon sugar

The secret is "don't over cook the asparagus." Here's how we do it.

1. In a large (6–7 quart) pot, bring a gallon of water to a boil.
2. Add a tablespoon of salt and a tablespoon of sugar. The sugar helps to strengthen the asparagus cell walls so that as gases escape during cooking, the chlorophyll will not leak out and turn your asparagus army green.
3. Trim off the bases of the asparagus—the large ones are tougher at the base. Peel them with a regular vegetable peeler so they will cook evenly.
4. Add asparagus to water. Once your water returns to a gentle boil, 3–5 minutes is a good rule of thumb for cooking time. It will vary with the size of the asparagus.
5. Next prepare an iced water bath to shock the asparagus and stop the cooking process.
6. Just before you think they are done, remove asparagus from the heat and drain. (All right, unless you spend a lot of time with asparagus, that may be a vague instruction. If the truth be known, we usually throw in a couple of extra spears to use to test doneness. When in doubt, underdone is better than overdone.)
7. After draining, place the asparagus into the ice bath and shock those shoots quickly. Leave in the iced water for the same amount of time as you cooked them.

Blood Orange Vinaigrette

1/4 bunch parsley
3 slices fresh ginger, about the size of a nickel
1 egg
1 1/2 cups blood orange juice
3 tablespoons champagne vinegar
4 tablespoons raspberry vinegar
3/4 cup granulated sugar
1 1/2 teaspoon salt

1. Combine in blender—parsley, ginger and egg—and blend on high.
2. Add orange juice, vinegars, and sugar and blend again.
3. Taste, and add salt if desired.
4. Arrange asparagus and fruit on plate and drizzle with dressing.

The bright tartness of the blood orange juice balances against the spring green of the asparagus with just a touch of sweetness from the berries.

Composed Fruit and Flower Salad

with Guava Coconut Vinaigrette
Serves up to 10

Because I was raised on sweet and pretty. –Duke Ellington (when asked why he was always upbeat and happy).

One of the special signatures of Hudson's is our herb and flower garden. Visitors to the restaurant can wander through the large garden, which sports a sign "Dogs and Deer Beware—Vicious Gardener." While deer are a real problem for local gardeners, we don't seem to be bothered by them. It may be our smoking 300 pounds of venison a week that keeps them away.

The key to the beauty of these herbs and flowers is strict adherence to the organic principles of gardening. Throughout the seasons, we incorporate organic compost along with blood and bone meals to enrich the beds that provide us with naturally beautiful garnishes to accompany our special style of food and flavors.

Part of the bacteria in this compost comes from the urine of ovulating cows. Jeff had just sprayed one day when Jay came tiptoeing through eating the sorrel— ah, would this be a new taste treat for the executive chef or would he be warned in time?

We love edible flowers, but edible does not necessarily mean delectable. The begonia is our favorite—crisp, tart, lemony flavor with lots of color. Nasturtiums are a close second—a rich and peppery flavor.

Here are a few other edibles: roses, dianthus, gardenia . . . borage, garlic, safflower . . . viola, violet, yucca . . .

nasturtium, begonia, geraniums . . . chives, marigolds . . . squash blossoms, gladiolus, lavender . . . day lilies, sunflowers, and hibiscus, also ornamental kale and banana flowers (blanch first though), plus all herb flowers. Fruit tree blossoms are good too— pear, apple, and peach, whatever is around in your garden.

"Hazy, Lazy Days of Summer"
—Nat King Cole

TIMING: Dressing can be done a day ahead. Everything else should be done "a la minute." Last minute preparation is the secret to an eye-appealing salad.

VARIATION: If your gardens aren't large enough to produce a bounty of "salad" then augment what you have with a chiffonade of butter lettuce.

The fruits are *your* choice. Because the dressing is somewhat tropical we tend to lean towards kiwi, pineapple, and bananas. A little julienned apple provides that Garden of Eden touch.

TOOLS:
Can Opener
Blender
Knife

Edible Flowers, Tropical Fruits

1. To create this salad, gather as many varieties of edible flowers as you wish and toss lightly in the Guava Coconut Vinaigrette. Don't forget the flowers of herbs and some late spring lettuces, as they will lend their own subtleties.
2. Arrange flowers and fruit on plate.
3. Drizzle with Guava Coconut Vinaigrette.

The most important part is to have fun and use your plate as a canvas. Build— paint—decorate with fruit and flowers.

Guava Coconut Vinaigrette
makes a quart or enough for 10 salads

1 cup guava paste
1 15-oz. can Coco Lopez—sweetened coconut milk
1 cup rice wine vinegar
1 teaspoon dark sesame oil
1 tablespoon garlic
1 tablespoon red onion, minced
1 tablespoon sugar
4 tablespoons ginger, minced
1/4 cup lime juice
3/4 teaspoon salt

1. Combine dressing ingredients in blender and process on high until smooth.
2. Drizzle over fruit.

A summer of flavors both sweet and tart.

Southwestern
Caesar Salad

Topped with Tabasco® Croutons and Smoked Shrimp

Serves 6

Jay spent part of his life cooking in New Orleans, (yes, that explains some of it) and as a kid used to play around making his own barbecue sauces. One day he came across one of those little bottles of Tabasco®—and started using it. The rest . . . is blistery.

Jay tends to put Tabasco® in everything, along with a little touch of vinegar—that's what he calls "the wang." But it's Courtney Swenson, our Executive Sous Chef (and resident spice girl—you've heard of cooking spice, haven't you?) who is responsible for these terrific croutons.

We use so much Tabasco® that we have taken out the plastic shaker tops so it can pour freely. It takes about a week to go through a gallon of red and only a little longer for the green version.

Working without the dasher spout is definitely living fearlessly, or is that dangerously? Once when we were doing a cooking school, what was supposed to be a dash turned into a fire-hose stream. We just smiled and said, "Oh, this will be the spicy version."

A spoonful of Tabasco® helps the medicine go down.

He chopped up peppers, mixed them with vinegar and Avery Island salt, put the mixture in wooden barrels to age, and funneled the resulting sauce into secondhand cologne bottles.
–James Conaway's description of Edmund McIlhenny's development of Tabasco® sauce

VARIATION: Be fearless in trying other flavored breads. At Hudson's we use a savory pumpkin bread or sometimes a garlic and black olive bread. Sourdough bread is terrific for flavor and really absorbs the Tabasco® butter.

TIMING: Dressing can be made 2–3 days ahead and kept refrigerated. Croutons take a long time but don't require a lot of supervision. Cooking can be interspersed with a good book or television.

TOOLS:
Blender
Propane Torch
Stove Top Smoker
Cookie Sheet

Southwestern Caesar Salad

24 smoked shrimp *(see Smoking section)*
2 heads of romaine
Tabasco® croutons

1. Remove the cover leaves of the romaine.
2. Quarter the heads.
3. Slice these quarters across into 1" widths. After cutting the romaine, wash and thoroughly drain the lettuce. Refrigerate.
4. To serve, toss lettuce with dressing, top with croutons and 4 smoked shrimp per person.

"Hot Stuff" —The Rolling Stones

Southwestern Caesar Dressing

1 cup parmesan cheese, freshly grated
3 large egg yolks
8 cloves garlic
2 shallots, peeled and chopped
8 anchovy fillets
2 tablespoons Dijon or Creole-style mustard
1 tablespoon balsamic vinegar
4 tablespoons fresh lime juice
1 jalapeno, seeded and diced
1/2 teaspoon ground cumin
1 1/2 cups olive oil
1 1/2 teaspoons salt

1. Combine all ingredients except oil and salt and purée in a blender.
2. Add the oil in a thin stream while blender is running.
3. Taste the dressing before adjusting any seasonings. The parmesan and anchovies provide a lot of saltiness.

Tabasco® Croutons

These croutons are time consuming but well worth the effort.

One large French bread baguette (day old slices better)
1/2 lb. butter
3 oz. Tabasco®
1 tablespoon granulated onion
1 tablespoon granulated garlic
2 each rosemary sprigs, fresh leaves only
3 each oregano sprigs, fresh leaves only
1 teaspoon salt

1. Cube your bread into 1/2" cubes.
2. Toast in the oven on a cookie sheet at 250° until dried, about 2 hours, turning every 30 minutes until dry.
3. To make the Tabasco® butter for the croutons, combine the rest of the ingredients in a small saucepan and bring to a boil.
4. Toss over croutons and arrange as a single layer on cookie sheet.
5. Bake at 250° for another hour, turning every 15 minutes.

The cumin and jalapeno really amp up a standard Caesar Salad. Combined with the piquant butteriness of the croutons and the smoked shrimp on top, it makes all your taste buds explode.

Garden Greens with Lime Basil Dressing

Topped with Pan-Seared Scallops
Serves 6

There are many different varieties of basil, all of which we grow, but for this dressing we use sweet Italian basil. Basil is a member of the mint family and grows easily in a pot or in the yard. In the winter months it can be grown successfully inside in a sunny window.

Squeeze and smell, rub some into your hand. It's kitchen aromatherapy. Nothing will brighten your spirits more than the smell of fresh basil.

Forward now, no holding back on that herb farming. A few years ago we added a second garden up on the roof of the shed to add to our herb supply. Once you build your confidence on herbs, lettuces are next . . . then raising a dairy cow for the cream in this recipe . . . but that's much later.

Lettuces for our salads vary quite a bit, but we prefer to use a variety. For easy preparation you can purchase "Mesclun Mix" at many supermarkets. These mixes contain a variety of young greens such as arugula, mache, oak leaf, frizze, radicchio and sorrel. Butterleaf or boston lettuce is delicious, too! The most fun is shopping the produce market, trying different flavors and incorporating colors and textures.

"When I die, sprinkle my ashes on the basil bed." —Big Homey

"Up on the Roof"
—Carly Simon

VARIATION: Shrimp instead of scallops | **TIMING:** Dressing can be held several days in the fridge. Shake before using.

TOOLS:
Blender
Measuring Cups
Zester
Large Sauté Pan

Lime Basil Dressing

This recipe makes enough dressing for 8 salads plus a little extra

1/3 cup fresh basil leaves, packed tightly
2 limes—juice of 2, zest of 1
1 cup heavy cream
1/4 cup sugar
3 tablespoons honey
1/3 cup champagne herb vinegar
1 tablespoon shallots, diced
1 teaspoon garlic, minced
3/4 teaspoon salt

1. Grind basil with lime juice and zest in blender.
2. Add the rest of the ingredients and blend until smooth.

Roof top herb garden

Pan-Seared Scallops

2 scallops per salad

12 large scallops
Bronze Rub *(see Salt and Seasoning section)*
4 tablespoons olive oil

1. Season scallops with Bronze Rub.
2. Heat olive oil over medium-high heat—350°. Sear scallops for 2–3 minutes on each side or until well browned. If you like them better cooked all the way through—lower heat to medium and cook 4 minutes on each side. Set aside.

Garden Green Salad

Enough greens for six salads

1. To serve, shake the dressing well. We suggest tossing the salad with the dressing so all the leaves are coated. You'll actually use a bit less dressing than by pouring it on, but we're not counting calories today.
2. Slice scallops in half and serve atop chilled greens dressed with Lime Basil Dressing.

This dressing is so light and fresh it's like a kiss on your greens.

Chilled Lobster and Texas Dewberry Coleslaw

Serves 8

This will definitely be the fanciest, richest coleslaw you'll ever make. It's a gourmet treat—not a barbecue side dish. It's what you would serve Julia Child if she came to your backyard picnic.

A dewberry is a wild Texas springtime berry related to the blackberry or the boysenberry. It grows by the side of the road, along the railroad tracks. In fact, it grows all over Texas. You can't stop it. For years it was mostly used for making jelly or ice cream.

But in this recipe, we've raised it to new heights, blending it into Dewberry Vinaigrette. Its flavor is that of summer and the color mixes well with the purple cabbage, providing a great contrast to the bright white medallions of lobster. It's a visual and flavor treat.

Backyard picnic food likes to get dressed up, too.

"Summertime"
—the Janis Joplin version.

VARIATION:
A shrimp or a scallop would be a worthy substitute for lobster.

TIMING:
This slaw is best when dressed at the last minute. Because of the thinness of the vegetables, the acid in the dressing will wilt the salad. So again, dress it a la minute for the crisp texture. But the dressing can be prepared the day before and the slaw in the morning to use in the afternoon.

TOOLS:
Smoker
Chef's Knife
Blender
Skewers
Mandoline
Cutting Board

Chilled Lobster

Techniques for smoking lobster can be found in the Smoking section. Smoking the tail whole is better for cutting into medallions. An old trick to keep the tail from curling is to insert two skewers lengthwise through the underside of the tail. Season and smoke the lobster in the manner described.

It isn't necessary to serve the lobster piping hot, so leave the skewers in until the lobster cools enough to handle. When cool, pull the skewers and slice into medallions across the length of the tail. Arrange the medallions against the slaw for that dramatic color effect.

1/2 head green cabbage, shredded
1 head red cabbage, shredded
1 carrot, julienned
1 jicama, julienned
1 red onion, julienned
1 red bell pepper, julienned
2 lobster tails (8 oz. tails)

1. Shred and julienne vegetables. Go for thinness and length. We like to use the mandoline for this job where we can. It works well on the cabbages, carrots, jicama and onion. Your sharpest chef's knife and a cutting board will be for the bell pepper.
2. Toss vinaigrette over mixed cabbages mounded on a plate and arrange lobster medallions atop the salad.

Texas Dewberry Vinaigrette

1/4 cup lime juice
1/4 cup raspberry vinegar
1 cup sugar
2 tablespoons garlic, minced
2 tablespoons shallots, minced
2 pints dewberries, loganberries or blackberries
1/4 cup sunflower oil
1 teaspoon salt
1/2 teaspoon white pepper

1. Combine lime juice, raspberry vinegar and sugar for dressing in a saucepan. Bring to a boil for 2–3 minutes to dissolve the sugar.
2. Combine garlic, shallots and dewberries in a blender and purée until smooth.
3. Add sugar syrup, oil, salt and pepper to the berry mixture and chill.

The richness of lobster, offset by the tangy crisp slaw screams summertime.

Jicama and Tomatillo Salad

with Gingered Lime Vinaigrette

Serves 6

After a week long skiing vacation in Santa Fe, Jeff's challenge was to clean out the refrigerator and feed six people. He had a couple of bunches of cilantro, a couple of fingers of ginger and some limes. In the crisper there were tomatillos, jicama and a carrot. Hmm . . . he said to himself. What does this want to be? As it turns out, that little thrown-together salad grew up to become the winner of the Texas Hill Country People's Choice Award.

It's a scene stealer—a side dish that sometimes gets more attention than the entrée. And it is that rarity for a Hudson's recipe—zero calories of fat. It was strictly by mistake, we guarantee.

TIMING: Make the dressing a day or two before, and the salad in the afternoon for evening use.

TOOLS:
Blender
Peeler
Mandoline or Knife

Gingered Lime Vinaigrette

1 1/2 cup fresh lime juice
1/2 cup champagne vinegar
3 tablespoons garlic, minced
1 tablespoon shallots, minced
1/2 cup sugar
4 tablespoons ginger, chopped
1/2 teaspoon salt

1. Combine all ingredients in a blender. Blend thoroughly .

Sometimes the things that are meant to be together are hiding at the back of your refrigerator.

Jicama and Tomatillo Salad

12 tomatillos, husks removed and quartered
2 large jicama, julienned
1 cup carrots, julienned
2 bunches cilantro, leaves only

1. Prepare tomatillos, jicama, carrots, and cilantro.
2. Dress salad with vinaigrette and toss.

"Happy Together" —*The Turtles*

Pucker, squirt
and crunch.

SOUPS— HOT AND COLD

Play with your Food.

Pheasant Tortilla Soup

Green Apple and White Bean Soup with Poblanos and Smoked Bacon

Oyster Stew Laced with Cilantro Pesto

Green Chili Corn Crawfish Soup

Avocado Soup with Mexican Marigold Pico de Gallo

Butternut Squash and Granny Smith Apple Soup Topped with Jerked Pumpkin Seeds

Green Gazpacho Soup with Red Pepper Paint

Poteet Strawberry and Fredricksburg Peach Soup in Frozen Flower Bowls

Duck Gumbo—Secrets of the Roux

Pheasant Tortilla Soup

Serves 8 generously

The inspiration for this soup came from a trip Jeff made to the small rustic resort town of Kaillum on the Caribbean. It's about 50 miles south of Cancun and at least that far from phones, electricity, or clocks. There he ate and cooked with three families who were the most happy, carefree people he had ever met. They used sign language and laughter to communicate, since they spoke a blend of Mayan and Spanish that only a few still understand.

Jeff was welcomed into a sand-floor kitchen, which smelled of achiote, cilantro and lime juice. One of the best things about it was how they cleaned the floor—kicked a little new sand over it and every 2 or 3 days raked it—another step toward the ultimate self-cleaning kitchen.

This Pheasant Tortilla Soup is based on their garlic, lime, cilantro, and chicken soup. At Hudson's we always have an abundance of pheasant stock since we are boning whole pheasants at least twice a week, but when hunting down bird carcasses for stock, chicken is much easier to find than pheasant and is less expensive. Chicken tortilla soup made by following this recipe is also tasty—just not as exotic.

VARIATIONS: Garnish with fried corn tortilla strips, shredded Jack cheese and salsa.

TIMING: Have the stock ready. Grill the bird a day ahead. Just wait to chop it until after it's cooled so the juices stay in. Soup can be made ahead, but add lime juice and cilantro ten minutes prior to serving to insure brightness of color and taste.

TOOLS:

Mandoline or Sharp Knife

Food Processor

Heavy-bottomed Stock Pot

Pheasant Tortilla Soup

1/2 cup fresh lime juice, Must be fresh!
1 1/2 cups cilantro, leaves only
1 1/2 cups grilled or smoked pheasant or chicken meat, pulled off the bone and cut into bite-size pieces
1 quart pheasant or chicken stock
5 ribs of celery, diced in 1/4" dice
1 cup red onion, minced
1 1/2 cups fresh sweet kernel corn (frozen corn is OK)
1/2 cup carrots, julienned (use a mandoline to make this easy)
1/2 cup garlic, minced in food processor
1 poblano pepper, roasted, peeled, seeded and diced in 1/4" dice
1 jalapeno, minced (for spicy leave in the seeds)
1 1/2 tablespoons salt

1. Set the lime juice, cilantro and the cooked pheasant to the side to be added in the final 5 minutes before serving.
2. Add all the other ingredients to a large heavy-bottomed stock pot and bring to a rolling boil.
3. Reduce to a simmer for about 30 minutes.
4. Add the lime, cilantro, and pheasant and return to a simmer and serve.

Concentrating on your stock and the freshest ingredients available will insure the best soup around.

See our Stock Options section for poultry stock recipe. Stock can be made a day or two ahead of time. The stock can be made in large amounts and stored in the freezer for other recipes.

"Mexico"
—James Taylor

This soup is like a blast of sunshine. The bright color, clear broth, and heat from the peppers are a warm Mexican afternoon in a bowl.

Butternut Squash and Granny Smith Apple Soup

Topped with Jerked Pumpkin Seeds

Serves 6–8

For seven pretty exciting years, Jeff had a restaurant in Aspen, where he was exposed to exotic people and flavors, good times and bad influences. One of those was the French liqueur, Pernod, with its rich complex licorice taste, both sweet and bitter. It lends a distinct grown-up flavor to this soup.

We traditionally serve this soup at the restaurant with Thanksgiving offerings. Years ago we began making a version of it minus the apples. One year we discovered that adding apples makes the soup a real stand out. We garnish the top of the soup with julienned apples and seasoned, toasted pumpkin seeds. Having a rich poultry stock is very important. *(See Stock Options section.)*

Acorn or other winter squash can be used in this recipe, but the butternut has the best meat-to-seed ratio. You'll find as you roast these winter squash that they'll brown on the pan side. As you're removing the meat from that side, taste it, and see how naturally rich and sweet the squash is.

VARIATION: Pernod may not be on hand or to your taste, so sherry will do nicely as a substitute, or even ouzo.

TIMING: This soup can be made the day before. Gently warm before service.

TOOLS:
Roasting Pan
Fork
Blender
Heavy Bottomed Sauce Pot
Peeler
Mandoline

Butternut Squash and Granny Smith Apple Soup

1 butternut squash
4 medium Granny Smith apples, peeled, cored and sliced (reserve one for garnish)
2 quarts of poultry stock, reduced to 2 cups, hot
1/4 teaspoon nutmeg
1/4 teaspoon cinnamon
6 tablespoons Pernod
1/2 cup heavy cream
1 1/2 tablespoons salt
1 teaspoon white pepper
Jerked Pumpkin Seeds

1. Preheat oven to 375°.
2. Cut the stems from the squash and place squash in a roasting pan.
3. Set in oven for 1 hour and 15 minutes or until the necks of the squash are tender. Use a fork to check for doneness. It should pierce the skin and squash should feel soft.
4. Cool for 30 minutes or so, until you can handle squash.
5. Cut in half lengthwise and remove the meat of the squash. Discard seeds and skin.
6. In batches, combine squash with peeled and cored apples and hot poultry stock in a blender. Purée until smooth. It will take several times to blend all the apples and squash.

Caution, if you are using hot poultry stock, remember the steam will expand, lifting the blending level and spraying the liquid on you and the kitchen. Hold the vented lid down with a dry kitchen cloth.

7. Transfer the squash/apple purée to a heavy-bottomed sauce pot
8. Add the nutmeg, cinnamon, Pernod and cream, and simmer for 15–20 minutes over medium heat. Stir often because thick soups need movement.
9. Taste and add salt and pepper.
10. Serve piping hot topped with a garnish of julienned apples and jerked pumpkin seeds.

Pumpkin Seeds

1 1/2 cups pumpkin seeds
3 tablespoons melted butter
1/3 cup Dry Jerk Seasoning *(see Salt and Seasoning section)*

1. Preheat oven to 250°
2. Toss all ingredients together and bake in an oven for one hour, turning and tossing at 15 minute intervals.

"Autumn"
—George Winston

Blends the tartness of the apples and the mellow richness of roasted butternut squash.

Green Gazpacho Soup

with Red Pepper Paint

Serves: 8–10

It's a soup. It's a dip. It's a great green salsa.

This soup has no peppers in it. It is cool in spice and temperature, but a couple of jalapeños would definitely complement it. This soup is best when served ice cold—on the other hand we have served it hot with good results.

Hot, cold, spicy or not, top it with this highlight sauce for a great taste. Feel free to express your artistic talents when painting with the sauce. It's a bit chunky so think Jackson Pollack.

The tomatillo, aka Mexican tomato, has hints of lemon and herbs and is the base for almost all green Mexican sauces and salsas.

Play with your food!

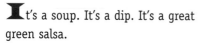

"First you say you will and then you won't" — Undecided Now

VARIATION:
Yes! Make up your own mind.

TIMING:
Paint can be prepared ahead of time.

TOOLS:
Food Processor
Blender
Wire Sieve or
Strainer
Squirt Bottles

Green Gazpacho with Red Pepper Paint

30 tomatillos, husked
1 red onion, rough chopped
3 cloves garlic, rough chopped
2 cucumbers, peeled and seeded, rough chopped
3 bundles cilantro, leaves only (toss the stems)
juice of 4 limes
1/2 cup virgin olive oil
3 oz. sherry vinegar
2 tablespoons sugar
jalapeño or serrano chilies (optional)
1 tablespoon salt or more

1. Combine ingredients and purée in a food processor.
2. Chill thoroughly and garnish with Ancho Red Bell Pepper Paint.

Ancho Red Bell Pepper Paint

2 ancho peppers, seeded and soaked in water to soften
1 red bell pepper, roasted and seeded
1 cup sour cream (or low fat yogurt, if you insist)
1 teaspoon salt

1. Combine ingredients in blender and purée until smooth.
2. Push through a sieve to smooth out the solids.
3. Load into plastic ketchup/mustard squirt bottles and release the artist in you—paint your plate!

Look up the word "tangy" in the Fearless dictionary and you'll see this soup.

Poteet Strawberry and Fredricksburg Peach Soup

in Frozen Flower Bowls
Serves 8–10

We think of this as the Tool Time Special—the best excuse there is for having duct tape and a blowtorch in the kitchen. We like to prepare this as a team with dueling blenders. It's an easy recipe that looks difficult. So feel free to show off.

When buying fruit, the riper the better. Our friend (his name is Curly) at the Peach Stand loves to see us coming. We buy all the overripe peaches that he can't sell to anyone else—a blemish or two is alright. Looks mushy? Tastes good.

Each kind of soup needs to be prepared separately, placing all ingredients into the blender and puréeing until smooth—then repeat with the other fruit and ingredients.

Note: Poteet and Fredricksburg are two small burgs in central Texas known for their flavorful fruits.

Bright, colorful food alerts the tastebuds they're in for a treat.

"Really like your peaches, wanna shake your tree," "The Joker" —Steve Miller Band

VARIATION: Return to blender, add 3 oz. of rum and have a fresh fruit daiquiri.

TIMING: Ice bowls usually need overnight to freeze, but can be done further in advance if you have the freezer space. Refrigerate soups for at least 3 hours or until well chilled. This can be done a day ahead if needed.

TOOLS:
Metal or Ceramic Bowls
Duct Tape
Blow Torch
Carafes or Pitchers
Blenders

Strawberry Soup

3 cups strawberries, cleaned with greens removed
1 cup chardonnay
1 1/2 cups fresh lemon juice
1 cup sugar, approximately*
1/2 cup cream

Peach Soup

3 cups peaches, skin on, no pits
1 cup chardonnay
1 1/2 cups fresh lemon juice
1 cup sugar, approximately*
1/2 cup cream
Mint for garnish

1. Combine all ingredients for strawberry soup in a blender and purée until smooth. Pour into carafe and hold in refrigerator until you are ready to serve. Clean blender.
2. Combine all ingredients for peach soup in blender and purée until smooth. Pour into carafe and hold in refrigerator until you are ready to serve.
3. Using two carafes, simultaneously pour into an ice bowl and garnish with mint.

Note: With very ripe fruit you can cut back on the sugar added because there is more natural sugar in the fruit.

Ice bowls

This frozen soup bowl gets the most ooohs and aaahs for presentation.

It's fun and simple. The only thing you need is a little extra freezer space. These bowls not only look great, they keep the soup chilled and there are no dishes to wash.

Not in the mood to make a bunch of small bowls? This is even more fun served in one big ice bowl—family style.

Water
Edible flowers

1. Fill a metal or ceramic bowl 3/4 full with water and edible flower petals, for example, rose, pansy, sunflower, etc.
2. Place a smaller bowl inside the first bowl and anchor with duct tape to keep it centered.
3. Freeze bowls overnight.
4. When ready to serve, remove duct tape and small bowl. Flash the larger bowl with a blow torch to release the finished ice bowl. (You don't have to use a blow torch. Room temperature will release the bowls in 10 to 15 minutes.)

Nothing is sweeter than summer fruits at their peak of ripeness.

Duck Gumbo
Secrets of the Roux

Serves 10–12

Dark, rich, and spicy, just like New Orleans.

It's usually about Halloween when that uncontrollable urge to make gumbo comes along. Maybe it's the first breath of cool north air blowing through Austin, or maybe it's something about the full moon. Like all Cajun food, gumbo's two influences are French and African. African-style gumbo is thicker and flavored with okra—and French gumbo is thickened with a dark chocolate brown roux. Some gumbo purists think that the two should never mix—ha! Not in this kitchen. Remember gumbo is one of those everything-but-the-kitchen-sink, refrigerator-cleaning recipes.

We have judged more than our share of gumbo cooking contests and therefore have tasted a lot of bad gumbo. There are as many variations as there are Cajuns.

We are partial to this recipe—just because we made it. So make your own adjustments, change crawfish to shrimp or crab or oysters, or presto change-o—duck to chicken, or goose.

Lean close now, here's the secret. On those magical occasions when we have experienced good gumbo, it almost universally had two ingredients that set it apart—a good dark roux, and a rich high-quality poultry stock base. *(Refer to the Stock Options section.)*

Finger Tip—Don't taste the roux with your finger. It's about 400° when it is reaching the right color. It looks and smells so good, it's just a natural reaction to stick your finger in. Ouch!

A wise man once said, "Any sufficiently advanced technology is indistinguishable from magic." We think this applies to gumbo as well.

VARIATION: As long as your stock and your roux are true almost anything goes: alligator, crawfish, squirrel, nutria, oysters, every kind of seafood, reptile, turtles, water moccasin and game imaginable. All substitutions are legal.

TIMING: The flavor will improve if served the second day because most good dark rouxs have a bit of bitterness that dissipates overnight.

TOOLS:
Heavy Bottomed Pot
Iron Skillet
Roasting Pan with Rack

"Yellow Moon"
—Neville Bros.

Duck Gumbo

- 1 store-bought duck (about 5 lbs.), or two wild ducks
- 3/4 cup duck fat (sounds like the name of a Chinese mobster)
- 3/4 cup flour
- 1/2 cup okra, fresh or frozen
- 3 tablespoons garlic, minced
- 2 cups onion, diced
- 2 cups celery, diced
- 1/2 cup poblano pepper, diced
- 2 quarts poultry stock
- 1/4 cup filé powder
- 4 bay leaves
- 1 teaspoon oregano
- 1 teaspoon thyme
- Tabasco® to taste (4–5 good shakes should do it)
- 1/4 cup Worcestershire sauce
- 2 tablespoons salt
- 1 tablespoon cayenne pepper (a little less if you're feeling heat wimpy)
- 1 teaspoon black pepper
- 1/2 lb. crawfish
- 1/2 lb. andouille or keilbasa sausage, sliced
- 1 cup tomatoes, 1/4" dice
- 4 cups cooked rice, cooked and set aside

1. Place duck on a roasting rack in a roasting pan in a 350° oven for about 20 minutes per lb. (approximately 1 hour and 45 minutes). The duck will finish cooking in the gumbo itself.
2. Remove duck from oven and pour off the fat, reserving 3/4 of a cup.
3. Let duck cool for 30 minutes until you can comfortably handle it. Pull the meat off the bone and set aside, discarding the skin.
4. To make the roux, bring duck fat to smoking point and slowly add flour. Stir flour and fat until the roux becomes a chocolate brown.

    Stir constantly making sure all flour is being blended. The flour will begin to cook and a wonderful smell will envelop your head. (I like it as much as the perfume of fresh bread baking.) Here's the trick—cook the flour to a rich chocolate brown without making the roux taste burnt. This takes some time and experience—but it's not brain surgery. Just remove from the heat and stir—and then return to the heat—back and forth.
5. Remove the roux from the heat and pour into a stock pot. Stir in the okra, garlic, onion, celery, and peppers.
6. Pour in the rich poultry stock and simmer over medium-low heat while you stir in all the spices.
7. Simmer for one hour on low heat. Taste for salt-pepper.
8. Add crawfish, sausage, tomatoes and duck meat.
9. Simmer for 30 minutes and adjust seasoning.
10. Serve atop hot rice.

The chemistry of roux

(for those who aren't content with magic):

As your roux cooks, you are toasting the gluten (the thickening agent in flour). If you don't, your gumbo will have a pasty consistency from the uncooked flour. The gumbo will also over thicken because uncooked gluten has a much higher thickening power.

FISH AND CRUSTACEANS

Some people march to the beat of a different drummer, other people tango.

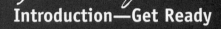

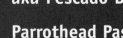

Introduction
Get Ready

Every good restaurant chef has his own philosophy and cooking technique when it comes to seafood. We enjoy delicate light flavors as much as the next guy—but our seafood, like our other cooking, is BIG and FEARLESS. We go for big, bold strokes and flavors—Smoke, Live Fires, and Southwestern Spices.

If the fish smells like the sea—a whiff of salty ocean spray—it's fresh.

Get fresh!

If it's fresh and comes from the sea—get ready for a taste that's naturally mild, sweet and good! That is if you season and cook with the right ingredients and techniques. But first—a few tips on how to get the freshest seafood to your kitchen.

1. **Shop at a busy seafood market.** This insures a quick inventory turnover and, thus, fresher seafood.

2. **Get to know the people behind the counter.** Strike up a conversation. Important questions to ask are: "What's the freshest? What came in today? What new whole fish arrived this morning? What's in season or running?"

3. **Practice the lost art of a thank-you note with gratuity** if what he or she sold you last week was especially fresh and delicious. Perfect this technique and you will be treated as royalty.

4. **Select whole fish packed on ice whenever possible**. The melting ice washes the bacteria off the seafood, so fillets fresh cut from whole fish are always the best.

5. If the fish smells like the sea—a whiff of salty ocean spray—it's fresh. If it smells like fish—it's not your dish.

6. Whole fish should have these qualities: red gills, bright eyes (the cloudier the eye, the older the fish) and shiny bright color throughout.

7. Filleted fish are trickier. Look for: No fish smell, bright color and firm texture, packed on top of ice—not wrapped in plastic.

So fasten your seat belts, limber up those tastebuds, 'cause they're going to get a work-out.

Trust the Crust

When we cook fillets we like to make a crust to add some crunchiness and a layer of texture to protect the fish. As it cooks, the fillet steams inside the crust for a lighter, flakier result. Yum!

For the next three recipes we give you variations on our "Trust the Crust" policy. All use the same basic breading procedure.

1. Pulse breading ingredients in a food processor to a medium coarse texture.

2. In a flat baking dish, combine the eggs and milk, lightly whisk to create the egg wash.

3. Place 1 cup all purpose flour in a flat baking dish. Next, dust the fish fillet in the flour.

4. Pass floured fillet through the egg wash, wetting the entire fillet.

5. Place fillet in crust mixture. Lightly press the mixture onto both sides of the fillet with the palm of your hand. Remove and shake off excess. Set aside on a dry sheet pan or cookie sheet until all the fillets are breaded.

Seafood oil cookery has unfairly been given a bad rap. Yes, we've all had greasy fried seafood— pffaah! The truth is, when done properly, very little of the cooking oil is absorbed into the food. There's no reason for it to be greasy.

Our crusted fillet recipes use different types of oil in varying amounts, but the basics are the same. We always heat the oil to 325° to 350°. Yes, you can use an oil or candy thermometer to be sure, but with experience you will be able to tell by just looking when the temperature is right. Here's what to look for:

1. Heat the oil over medium-high heat until it begins to shimmer–like the heat waves coming off a Texas blacktop road in August.

2. Or, drop a leaf of parsley, cilantro, or even a blade of grass into the oil. If the temperature is right, it will sizzle and pop.

3. If the oil begins to smoke, it's too hot. Reduce your heat.

Once the oil is the right temperature, you're on your way. Here are a few more tips to insure good results.

1. Do not overload your pan with what you are cooking. This drops the cooking temperature and causes the food to suck up the oil and get greasy.

2. Use a heavy-bottomed skillet to hold the heat and maintain proper temperature.

3. And our favorite technique– cook a small piece first and taste it.

If any of this sounds complicated–fear not! Once you've done it once or twice you'll get the hang of it.

Hot and Crunchy
Trout

with Mango Jalapeño Aioli

Serves 6–8

Every good restaurant has one or two items on the menu that people order time and time again, or sometimes they complain that they would like to order something different, but they just have to order this . . . they can't help themselves. At Hudson's, this is the one.

Like the best recipes at Hudson's, this came from collaboration. Courtney Swensen, our Sous Chef, had created this delight at another restaurant with a different sauce that had to be cooked in the same pan as the fish. Not a bad sauce, but cumbersome when preparing a couple of hundred meals in an evening. We suggested she pair it up with the Mango Jalapeño Aioli and voilà—a match made in heaven.

When Dan Rather escapes world crises long enough to visit his lakeside home near us, he will often wander in and order this dish. He likes it so much that he asked us to fix it at his house for a party. For his wife's birthday, we modified it slightly to make *her* favorite, Hot and Crunchy Prawns.

Experience the difference that texture makes.

"Gone Fishin'"
—Louie Armstrong & Bing Crosby

VARIATION: This breading mixture can be used on other seafood and meats with wonderful results. Just be sure that the fish, meat, or vegetable is cut thin enough to be cooked in just a few minutes on each side. Otherwise the breading will over brown. It's wonderful on a thin chicken breast.

TOOLS:

Food Processor
Large Skillet for Sautéing
Cookie Sheet
3 Flat Dishes for Breading Materials
Turning Spatula
Whisk

Hot and Crunchy Trout

6 to 8 trout fillets, 8 oz. each
1/4 cup almonds
1/4 cup sesame seeds
2 cups cornflakes
1/4 cup granulated sugar
1 1/2 tablespoons red chili flakes
1 tablespoon salt
1 cup milk
2 eggs
1 cup all purpose flour
6 tablespoons clarified butter

1. Toast almonds and sesame seeds separately in a dry skillet until lightly toasted. Set aside to cool.
2. Combine almonds, sesame seeds, cornflakes, sugar, red chili flakes, and salt in a food processor and pulse until coarse and crunchy but well blended. Empty onto platter or baking sheet.
3. Whisk milk and eggs to make egg wash.
4. Put flour in a flat dish. Then, holding the trout fillet by the tail, dredge it in the flour until well dusted. Pat off excess flour.
5. Pass dusted fillet through the egg wash, wetting the entire fillet.
6. Place fillet in hot and crunchy mixture, lightly pressing the mixture on the fillet with the palm of your hand. Remove and shake off excess. Set aside on a dry sheet pan or cookie sheet until all the trout are breaded.

7. In a large, heavy sauté pan, heat 6 tablespoons clarified butter to about 325° until it shimmers, or until parsley sizzles when tossed in.
8. Lay the trout fillet in the hot pan skin-side up. Sauté for about 3 minutes on each side. It will cook to a golden crunchy brown. Turn the fillet only once.
9. Place each fillet on a cookie sheet in a warm oven (180°) until you have completed this process for all the fillets. If you are lucky enough to have a griddle in your kitchen, you can cook 3 or 4 fillets at the same time.

TIMING: Make sauce and breading the day before.

The crunch of the nut crust and the spice from Mexico collide in your mouth.

The Mango Jalapeño Aioli is a light fruity sauce that offsets the spice from the breading mixture. You can make it from scratch from the second recipe below or order the Mango Jalapeño sauce from Hudson's by calling 1-800-996-7655. We won't tell.

Mango Jalapeño Aioli—The Easy Way

Juice of 2 lemons
1 bunch cilantro, leaves only, rough cut
1/2 cup Hudson's Mango Jalapeño Sauce
1 cup mayonnaise
2 cloves garlic, minced
Salt and pepper to taste, about
    1/2 tablespoon

Combine in a bowl and whisk until well blended.
    We place the Mango Jalapeño Aioli on the plate first, with the fish on top.

Mango Jalapeño Sauce—The Fearless Way

1 lb. mangoes, diced
1 1/2 cups granulated sugar
3 oz. champagne vinegar
2 tablespoons garlic, minced
3 tablespoons red onion, diced
4 jalapeños, seeded and sliced
1/2 teaspoon salt

1. Combine mangoes, sugar, vinegar, garlic and red onion. Bring to a boil.
2. Reduce to a simmer and cook 10 minutes.
3. Add jalapeños and salt.
4. Serve the sauce hot or cold. If making aioli, chill completely before adding to other ingredients.

Pecan Crusted Red Snapper

Atop Lemon Herb Sauce

Serves 6

This entrée was on the menu the first day Hudson's opened in 1984. It seemed a natural since there was a pecan tree in the backyard. Talk about indigenous—it was the natural nut to use.

For nine years this dish was a perennial favorite before it was nudged off the menu by Hot and Crunchy Trout. It still makes an occasional guest appearance as a tasty old friend. In 1986, the recipe was printed in *Gourmet Magazine* by reader request.

Snapper has a mild, light flavor and is a good fish for people who don't like a strong fishy flavor or "fish for people that don't like fish."

That's the whole kettle of fish in a nutshell.

"In the Summertime" —*Mungo Jerry*

VARIATIONS: How many nuts are there in the world? Pine nuts to pistachios, macadamias. Chef's nuts roasting on an open fire.

TIMING: The pecan crust breading of the fish can be done the morning of the dinner. Store the breaded fillets between wax paper in the refrigerator until cooking time.

TOOLS: Food Processor, Frying Pan, Spatulas, 3 Flat Dishes for Breading Materials, Saucepan, Knife, Blender, Skillet or Sauté Pan

Pecan Crust Breading

1 cup bread crumbs
2 cups pecan pieces
1 teaspoon each: dried basil, dried oregano, whole leaf thyme, granulated garlic, granulated onion, white pepper

1. Pulse all breading ingredients in a food processor until medium fine.
2. Then put on a flat dish and set aside.

Pecan Crusted Red Snapper

6 boned snapper fillets, 6–8 oz. each, approximately 1/2" thick
2 eggs
1 cup milk
1 cup flour
1 cup olive or canola oil

1. In a flat dish, combine the eggs and milk. Whisk to create the egg wash.
2. Put flour in a flat dish. Then, holding the trout fillet by the tail, dredge it in the flour until well dusted. Pat off excess flour.
3. Pass floured fillet through the egg wash, wetting the entire fillet.
4. Place fillet in pecan meal breading mixture. Lightly press the mixture onto both sides of the fillet with the palm of your hand. Remove and shake off excess. Set aside on a dry sheet pan or cookie sheet until all the fillets are breaded.

4. Heat oil in large skillet or sauté pan over medium-high heat until it shimmers. Sauté fillets until golden brown. Sauté in batches of 2 or 3, so the oil does not cool down.

Spring Lemon Herb Sauce

This is a light, thin sauce that will hold for 30 minutes only.

1 cup chardonnay or white wine
1 shallot, minced
4 cloves garlic, minced
2 cups good chicken stock, reduced to 1 cup
1 cup mixed fresh lemon herbs: lemon balm, lemon thyme, sorrel, lemon basil, begonias
1 1/2 teaspoons salt or more
1/2 teaspoon white pepper
3/4 lb. (3 sticks butter), cubed 1" and chilled

1. In a saucepan, reduce wine with garlic and shallots until almost dry.
2. Add reduced chicken stock and heat until boiling.
3. Add hot stock mixture and herbs to the blender and turn on high. Be careful. Cover top with towel and let expanded steam release.
4. Quickly add butter, 3 to 4 chunks at a time until all is in solution.
5. Add salt and white pepper.

Red
Snapper
is one of the
flakiest fish and
marries well with the
slight sweetness of the pecans and
the creamy citrus of the sauce.

Catfish in a Tortilla Corn Crust

Topped with Green Chili Tartar Sauce

Serves 6

In Austin, on Manchaca Road off Lamar Boulevard on any Friday night, you'll find a mess of catfish fryin' up in a big pot of boiling oil. It's fueled from a propane tank that makes a sound like a jet engine taking off. That's the Manchaca Fire Department having its Catfish Fry. These people are serious about their catfish—it's as traditional as Texas chili or barbecue. So don't catch fire in Manchaca on a Friday night!

Jay's Grandma Tims used to fry up catfish in cornmeal. The Hudson's variation spins off from there tastily and fearlessly with the addition of corn tortilla crust, cumin, chili powder and lemon pepper.

Some people march to the beat of a different drummer, other people tango.

"Where the catfish play" On Blue Bayou — Roy Orbison

VARIATIONS:
Bass, snapper, trout.

TIMING:
Make the Green Chili Tartar Sauce the day before. Mix crust and store in an air-tight container, if you want.

Catfish in a Tortilla Corn Crust

6 catfish fillets, 6–8 oz. each
4 cups crushed corn tortilla chips (Store bought corn tortilla chips are fine, preferably white. If salted, adjust seasoning accordingly.)
1/2 cup cornmeal
1 tablespoon cayenne
2 tablespoons dark chili powder
2 teaspoons ground cumin
2 tablespoons lemon pepper
1 tablespoon salt
2 tablespoons granulated garlic
2 eggs
1 cup milk
2 cups flour
3 cups peanut or vegetable oil

TOOLS:
10–12" Skillet or Deep Fryer
Food Processor
3 Flat Dishes for Breading Materials

1. Pulse tortilla chips gently in food processor until crumbled, but not dust. Crush, don't pulverize, for eye appeal and texture.
2. Toss tortilla chip crumbs, cornmeal, and seasonings, adjusting cayenne to your own taste.
3. In a flat dish, combine the eggs and milk, whisking to create the egg wash. Put flour in another flat dish.
4. Dredge fish through flour, then egg wash, then into seasoned chili corn crust mixture.
5. Pan fry in 1/2 inch of peanut or vegetable oil, about 2 minutes each side, turning fish only once. Or, if you prefer, deep fry the fillet. Cook in batches of three until crust is set and evenly browned. Keep oil temperature around 350°.

Green Chili Tartar Sauce

You'll also find this recipe in the appetizer section with the shrimp fritters, but fried catfish is heaven with this on top. The secret to this recipe is finding the right kind of green chili pepper—the long New Mexico or Texas chili is the best. A roasted Anaheim is a quality substitute, or a poblano pepper will work if you can't find Anaheims. They're a little hotter—

In this dish it's the contrast of textures—the rough, spicy crunchiness of the crust and the sweet tenderness of the fish plus the cool, sharp, lime-iness of the sauce.

about a 5 on a scale of 10. A lot of good groceries and gourmet shops now carry frozen roasted green chili peppers, which are also okay, if you can't get fresh.

2 cups mayonnaise
1/4 cup garlic, minced
1/4 cup capers, drained
3 bunches cilantro, leaves
  only
2 cups green chili peppers
1 red bell pepper, diced
5 limes, zest and juice

1. Blister and peel skin from peppers *(see Pepper section)*.
2. Cut them in half. Remove the seeds and veins, and dice into 1/4" pieces. Reserve the red pepper and an equal part of the green chili pepper for garnish.
3. The rest of the green chili pepper goes into the food processor with all the other ingredients and is pulsed to blend.
4. Chill and serve on top of fried catfish with green and red chili pepper garnish.

Grilling Fish

For enjoying the subtleties of fish flavor and the complexities of our salsas, nothing beats fish from the grill. Shark, tuna, mahi, swordfish and salmon are all excellent fish for grilling, due to their steak-i-ness. We recommend these "steak" fish for easy grilling because the grain of the flesh is large and won't flake into the coals. But don't limit yourself, ask your local seafood specialist for suggestions. With the advent of grilling baskets or cages, even the flakiest of fish can take to the grill for a memorable taste experience.

At the restaurant, we like our fish steaks about 3/4" to 1" thick. This keeps them moister because they're not too thin. They can stay on the grill a bit longer and develop a better grilled flavor. We like to calculate 7–8 minutes cooking time per inch of thickness. Then we check for doneness. If you see moisture drops on top of the fillet, that means it is sufficiently cooked, probably medium-well.

The one tricky thing about grilling fish that are low in fat, is that it's really easy to overcook.

TOOLS:
Having the right tool will make your life a whole lot easier—an 8" metal spatula for turning the fish on the grill is worth the investment.

When cooking over charcoal or a wood-fire grill, allow the coals to cool to a medium high heat. Fish cooked over a roaring fire will be charred on the outside and raw (not rare) inside.

Here are a few secrets to having those perfect grill marks on a perfectly cooked piece of fish.

1. Coat the fillet with one of the seasoning rubs or dust with flour. This light coating will help in releasing the fish from the grill.

2. Wipe the grill with an oiled towel before placing the fish down. This seasons the grill and provides added insurance against sticking.

3. Most important is to allow the fish some time on the grill to release naturally. It's always tempting to run your spatula under the fish, but be patient and allow it to sit. As the flesh lightly "chars", it will release itself, along the grill marks. This will occur after 3 minutes.

4. When grilling a fillet like salmon or mahi mahi, place it on the grill skin side up for 3 minutes to mark the fish, turn it 90 degrees for 2 minutes, then flip it skin side down to complete the cooking. Your fish now has beautiful grill marks and you don't have to worry about flipping it as it approaches doneness.

Shellfish on the Grill

When grilling shellfish—particularly shrimp and scallops—we employ the "Bigger is Better" (BIB) rule. These behemoths aren't readily available so plan ahead and speak with your new best friend—the fish monger—about getting some. At the restaurant we use large sea scallops and jumbo to huge shrimp. If you're concerned about the shrimp or scallops scattering on the grill, just skewer 'em. Not only does this get the shrimp "in line" but the togetherness on the skewer adds density and thus, moisture retention.

When cooking the shellfish on the grill, again, cook over medium to medium-high heat and cook until firm but not hard. If you break a shrimp open, for example, the flesh will be white. Break open a slightly underdone shrimp, and you'll see it is still opaque.

Now that you have the basics, you can add a variety of rubs, salsas and seasoned butters for your grilling enjoyment. Let freshness be your guide to selecting fish. Then you can choose the rub and sauce that suits your mood. Be fearless, mix and match.

When cooking shellfish we employ the (BIB) rule, "Bigger is Better."

Here are a few of our favorite combinations:

Grilled skewer of scallops and shrimp—basted with Sundried Tomato Tequila Chili Butter and served atop Fiery Peach Salsa

Grilled swordfish with Bronze Rub and Lime Zest Chardonnay Butter

Salmon with Bronze Rub topped with Tres Lemon Herb Butter

Grilled tuna dusted with Jerk Seasoning and topped with Green Tomato Relish

Mahi mahi dusted with Smoke Rub with Papaya Salsa (note the tropical theme—tropical fish, tropical sauce)

Grilled shark steak with Jerk Seasoning and Salsa Del Fuego—the rub and the salsa both have bite, as does a shark (try whistling Mack the Knife while you cook this one)

Ay - Here's the Rubs

Smoke Rub — a little bit salty but goes great with anything smoked on the grill.

1 cup paprika
1/3 cup onion powder
1/8 teaspoon cayenne
1/2 teaspoon white pepper
2 teaspoons dark chili powder
3 tablespoons brown sugar
1/2 cup granulated garlic
1 teaspoon curry
1/2 teaspoon black pepper
1/4 cup kosher salt

Combine and use freely to coat meat.

Bronze Rub — our favorite on many things, low salt, all purpose

1/2 cup of toasted and ground
   coriander seeds
1 tablespoon ground onion
3 tablespoons lemon pepper
1 tablespoon oregano, dried leaf
1 teaspoon white pepper
1 teaspoon black pepper
1 teaspoon cayenne pepper
1 tablespoon salt

Mix together in a food processor and use freely.

Jerk Season—Extremely Fearless

No, jerk season is not the time of year when certain chefs get full of themselves. It's a highly potent, lip tingling rub for smoking or grilling.

1 cup sugar
3/4 cup garlic powder
4 tablespoons salt
1 tablespoon white pepper
1 teaspoon allspice
1 tablespoon dry mustard
3/4 cup onion powder
1/4 cup thyme, dried whole leaf
1 tablespoon black pepper
1/2 tablespoon cayenne or 1/2 tablespoon habanero,
   ground
3 tablespoons curry
1/2 teaspoon clove

Combine ingredients. To use, coat meat with seasoning and smoke or grill.

The rubs can be kept in airtight containers at room temperature for several weeks.

Smoked Rainbow Trout with Bronze Rub p.88

Three Compound Butters and a Relish

These compound butters are a simple, yet very flavorful rich topping for any fish dish. They are best when squeezed out of a pastry bag into half-dollar-sized dollops or rosettes. They can easily be frozen then brought back to serving temperature for that last minute meal—just leave at room temperature for 7 minutes. Sauté shrimp or scallops in them for an easy but elegant dish. Each recipe makes enough for 8–10 portions.

Lime Zest Chardonnay Butter

1 cup white wine a good chardonnay or
   sauvignon blanc
1 tablespoon garlic, minced
1 tablespoon shallots, minced
2 juicy limes (3 if not juicy), zested and juiced
2 sticks sweet butter, chilled and cubed
1 teaspoon salt
1/2 teaspoon white pepper
1 bunch cilantro—leaves only, chopped

1. Combine wine, garlic and shallots in sauté pan. Reduce over heat until just a tablespoon of amber liquid remains.
2. Add lime zest and juice. Remove from heat and cool completely.
3. Combine wine reduction and butter in a food processor using the S-blade to blend.
4. Adjust seasoning with salt and white pepper and fold in cilantro.
5. Make into dollops or rosettes and refrigerate.
   They will hold for months in the freezer if wrapped properly.

Sundried Tomato Tequila Chili Butter

1 cup tequila
1/2 cup sundried tomatoes
2 tablespoons shallots, minced
1 tablespoon garlic, garlic
4 limes, zested and juiced
2 sticks sweet butter, chilled and cubed
2 tablespoons dark chili powder
1 teaspoon salt
1/4 tablespoon cayenne pepper
2 tablespoons sugar

1. Combine tequila, sundried tomatoes, shallots and garlic in a saucepan and simmer over medium heat. Be careful, the tequila can and may ignite and flame until the alcohol has burned off. When the liquid is almost gone, leaving about two tablespoons of golden liquid, remove from the heat and cool.
2. Add all the rest of the ingredients to the cooled mixture in a food processor and pulse with an S-blade until well blended.
3. Place in a pastry bag and squeeze out dollops or rosettes.

Tres Lemon Herb Butter

We recommend using a combination of any three of the following lemon scented plants: lemon basil– lemon balm– lemon thyme– lemon sorrel– lemon mint– lemon verbena– lemon scented flowers like begonias or lemon scented geraniums.

When you're in the fresh herb section of your store, do a little pinching and tasting—they won't mind—just pinch off a tiny piece of leaf and give it a taste.

The other secret to this is to reduce your wine down to an amber colored liquid until it's almost all gone.

1 cup quality white wine
1 tablespoon shallots, minced
2 lemons, zested and juiced
1/4 cup of minced herbs—your blend.
1 teaspoon salt
1/2 teaspoon white pepper ground
2 sticks sweet butter, chilled and cubed

1. Combine wine and shallots in a small saucepan and reduce to approximately 1 tablespoon amber liquid. Set aside to cool.
2. Add lemon juice, zest and herbs to wine and shallot mixture in a food processor with an S-blade and pulse until well blended. Add butter and blend well.
3. Place blended butter in a pastry bag, make into rosettes and refrigerate.

Green Tomato Relish

This is so good and you can do so much with it.

1 large sweet onion, 1/4" dice (try sweet onions such as Maui, Vidalia, or Texas 10/15)
2 lbs. green tomatoes, quartered
3 tablespoons garlic, chopped
2 tablespoons mustard seed
1 cup champagne vinegar
1 cup granulated sugar
1 tablespoon kosher salt
1 pinch white pepper
1 teaspoon Tabasco®
3 limes–juice and zest, minced–reserving zest for later
3 tablespoons cornstarch
2 tablespoons water
1 each poblano, red and yellow pepper, diced
1 cup kernel corn

1. Combine chopped onions, green tomatoes, garlic, mustard seed and vinegar in a sauce pot, cover and cook over medium heat until tomatoes are cooked but firm.
2. Transfer to a food processor and pulse to chop, taking care not to purée.
3. Return to heat and add sugar, salt, pepper and lime juice.
4. Bring to a boil and thicken with cornstarch dissolved in water.
5. Fold in zest, peppers and corn and cool.

Four Salsas

Green Chili Salsa

2 tablespoons coriander seeds, toasted and ground
1/2 yellow onion, large dice
4 tablespoons garlic, minced
3 tablespoons olive oil
1 quart tomatillos, husks removed and quartered
2 cups New Mexico green chili peppers (see Pepper section)
5 limes, juice and zest
3 tablespoons sugar
1 teaspoon salt
2 red bell peppers, small dice
1 bunch cilantro, leaves only

1. Toast coriander seeds in a small dry skillet over medium high heat, stirring constantly until lightly toasted. Set aside to cool.
2. Sauté onion and garlic in olive oil over medium-high heat.
3. Add tomatillos, green chilies, juice, zest and coriander seeds and cook until slightly thickened.
4. Add sugar and seasonings, transfer to food processor, and pulse to an even chunky consistency.
5. Add red bell peppers and cilantro, mix and refrigerate.

Papaya Salsa

6 tablespoons guava paste
1 tablespoon and 1 teaspoon sugar
1 lime, juice and zest
1/4 cup raspberry vinegar
1 papaya, diced (approximately 1 cup)
1 star fruit, diced
1 kiwi, peeled and diced
1 teaspoon garlic, minced
1 teaspoon shallots, minced
1/2 red bell pepper, small dice
1/2 jalapeño, minced
1 teaspoon salt

1. Combine guava paste, sugar, lime juice and zest and raspberry vinegar and liquefy in a blender.
2. Combine fruits and vegetables in a bowl and stir in guava dressing.
3. Adjust seasonings with salt and chill.

Fiery Peach Salsa

2 limes, zest and juice
1/2 cup raspberry vinegar
1 cup sugar
1 1/2 lbs. peaches, skinned and chopped
2 tablespoons garlic, minced
2 tablespoons shallots, minced
1/2 red onion, julienned
1/2 large red bell pepper, diced
4 jalapeños, julienned and seeded
2 tablespoons black peppercorns, cracked

1. Combine lime juice and zest, raspberry vinegar and sugar in a bowl. Stir to dissolve sugar.
2. Add all other ingredients to the bowl and mix gently. Refrigerate for two hours before serving but don't make it more than 6 hours ahead.
3. Toss gently—it's easy to mash this salsa into mush.

Salsa del Fuego

This salsa was created by our infinitely spicy Sous Chef Courtney Swenson. Courtney is a fifth generation Austinite, the only true native in our kitchen. The rest of us got here as quick as we could. Courtney's taste buds are not afraid of the heat that chili peppers bring to her cooking and that is reflected in this salsa. She created this to complement a grilled sea bass, but this salsa is so rich and flavorful it can improve almost anything it touches. The translation of Salsa del Fuego is, "sauce of the fireworks." This recipe not only includes smoking* the tomatoes and peppers, but also the charring of two tomatoes and a poblano pepper. Please believe us this sauce is not the same without the smoke and fire.

*See Smoking Section.

For the smoker: Cut the veggies below in half and clean the seeds, stems, and ribs from the peppers.

2 Roma or Mayan tomatoes
1 poblano pepper
2 red sweet bell peppers
1 jalapeño pepper
1 large yellow onion
3 tablespoons olive oil
3 tablespoons fresh lime juice
1 teaspoon Worcestershire
1/2 teaspoon green Tabasco®
1 teaspoon oregano, dry and chopped
1 tablespoon fresh lemon pepper
4 tablespoons coriander seeds, toasted and ground
2 jalapeños, seeded and minced
1 bunch green onions or scallions
1 bunch fresh cilantro, leaves only, rough cut
1 teaspoon granulated sugar
1 splash of your favorite tequila
Salt to taste (it may not need any)

1. Toast coriander seeds in a small dry skillet, stirring until lightly toasted. Cool and grind in a spice grinder or small food processor.
2. Cut the veggies in half and clean the seeds, stems and ribs from the peppers.

We suggest you combine the next two steps—smoking and charring.

3. In your smoker build a fire. At the peak of the fire take the 2 tomatoes and poblano pepper and char them over the open fire—don't be bashful—BURN 'EM. Turn them with metal tongs directly over the flame until all sides are black. Set them aside to cool.
4. After the fire has died down and is not flaming, place the red bell peppers, jalapeño and onion in the smoker, away from the direct heat. If you are using charcoal, smother the coals with water soaked wood chips and cover for 30 to 45 minutes, allowing the smoke to flavor all the vegetables. Remove from the smoker and place all smoked and charred ingredients in a food processor. Pulse until chunky but blended. Refrigerate.
5. In a large bowl combine the olive oil, fresh lime juice, Worcestershire sauce, green Tabasco®, oregano, lemon pepper, coriander seeds, jalapeños, green onions or scallions, cilantro, sugar and tequila.
6. Gently mix the smoked vegetables with the ingredients in the bowl and refrigerate. Salt to taste.

The translation of Salsa del Fuego is, "sauce of the fireworks."

Smoked Rainbow Trout

with Nopalitos, Smoked Bacon and Apple Jack Sauce

Serves 6

Nopalitos are the pads of the prickly pear cactus. Step one—go to the desert and pick cactus—just kidding. If you don't have access to these already cleaned, you'll get a similar taste and texture with green beans. We have actually seen canned nopalitos.

This dish was inspired by a secret that every chef knows—apples, bacon and onions want to be together. We just couldn't resist throwing in a cactus.

"They fried the fish with bacon and were astonished, for fish had never seemed so delicious before."
–Mark Twain

"She was all decked out, like a rainbow trout" —Gordon Lightfoot

VARIATION:
We also jar an apple cider brandy sauce *(see Resources section).*

TIMING:
Make sauce just prior to smoking the fish and bacon.

TOOLS:
Smoker, Medium
    Saucepan
Mandoline

Smoked Rainbow Trout with Nopalitos

6 trout fillets, 6–8 oz. each
1 lb. bacon
Bronze Rub *(see "Here's the Rubs" in this chapter)*

1. Dust trout with Bronze Rub and smoke until medium-rare to medium *(see Smoking section for techniques).* At the same time, smoke bacon to render off the fat and add smoke flavor.
2. Cut smoked bacon into 1/4" dice.

Apple Jack Sauce

1 6-oz. can of apple juice concentrate
1 tablespoon garlic, minced
1 tablespoon red onion
2 oz. Jack Daniels® whiskey
1 teaspoon salt
1/4 teaspoon white pepper
1 lb. smoked bacon
1 green apple, julienned (we recommend Granny Smith)
3 nopalitos, cleaned and julienned, or 2 cups green beans, pre-cooked to crunchy stage

1. In a saucepan, mix apple juice concentrate, garlic, onion, Jack Daniels®, and salt and pepper. Simmer for 10 minutes
2. Add smoked bacon, apple, and cactus. Simmer 1 minute. Top trout with sauce and serve.

A combination of smoky and tart, prickly and sweet.

Smoked Shrimp and Flounder en Papillote

aka Pescado Bota

Serves 2

This recipe started out as "Pompano en Papillote" around 1881 when it came from France to New Orleans to honor a famous balloonist. The idea was for the parchment paper to blow up like a balloon, perhaps to remind him of his vessel. Over time, our version of this dish has evolved from the French into more of a Mexican-style.

At Hudson's this is a popular entrée. On at least two separate occasions people have eaten the entire bag. We guess they wanted to get their money's worth.

What goes up, goes down nicely with the right sauce.

"Up, Up and Away" —The Fifth Dimension

VARIATION: What's in a name? Call it flounder, French turbot or Dover sole—it's all pretty tasty.

TIMING: Prepare the uncooked papillote up to 6 hours ahead (just refrigerate it).

TOOLS:
Scissors
Drinking Straw
Paper Clip
Baking Sheet
Parchment Paper

Smoked Shrimp and Flounder en Papillote

1 bottle of chardonnay
2 sheets parchment paper, 16 x 12 (to make the bag)
3 tablespoons butter, softened
2 teaspoons garlic, minced
2 tablespoons shallots, minced (substitute onion, leeks, celery or jicama as whimsy moves you)
2 flounder fillets, 5–6 oz. each
6 shrimp (21–25 per lb. size)
2 sprigs cilantro
2 sprigs thyme
2 teaspoons lime zest
1 roasted poblano, julienned
1/8 teaspoon salt
1/8 teaspoon pepper

1. Preheat oven to 350°. Put in baking sheet to preheat.
2. Reduce wine in a small saucepan to 1/2 cup.
3. Fold parchment paper in half to cut the heart and make it symmetrical. Repeat with the other sheet.
4. Butter the inside of each sheet thoroughly. Slightly off center on the paper, sprinkle garlic and shallots.
5. Top each parchment heart with flounder, shrimp, herbs, zest and poblano, divided equally.
6. Splash with reduced wine.
7. Season each with salt and pepper. Top with remaining butter.
8. Starting at the bottom, fold the edges over themselves (kind of like folding a note in high school) sealing the entire paper bag. One trick we sometimes use is to puff with a straw at one end of the bag to make sure it inflates, then hold it closed with a paper clip.
9. Place on pre-heated baking sheet.
10. Place in 350° oven for 9–10 minutes. Serve immediately.

These can also be prepared for a party with each person bagging their own fish. It's great fun.

The delicate paper steamer marries and carries the light fish in a sauce of mellow wine and zesty lime.

Parrothead Pasta

Serves 8

This seafood dish was a favorite of Jimmy Buffett's when he used to eat at our restaurant in Aspen, Colorado. We catered his bachelor party and rehearsal dinner, along with many other memorable evenings—oh, the stories we could tell. His music often accompanies us in the kitchen. He strikes us as a person who understands the concepts of adventure, not taking yourself too seriously, and living "fearlessly."

If you have a choice between not enough and too much, always choose too much.

"A Pirate Looks at 40" —Jimmy Buffett

VARIATION: You don't have to smoke the seafood, but if you add it raw, cook it a little bit longer.

TIMING: This dish is designed to be cooked just prior to serving so you need to have all your ingredients chopped and measured, ready to go. The French call this "mise in place"—essentially to have everything in place. It also makes you look very professional. No point in missing an opportunity to show off.

TOOLS:

14" Sauté Pan or Large Roasting Pan

Tongs

Parrothead Pasta

2 large smoked* lobster tails
24 large shrimp
24 large smoked scallops
1/2 lb. crabmeat
1/2 lb. dry spinach fettuccini
1/2 lb. dry egg fettuccini
2 cups white wine
1/4 cup olive oil
3 tablespoons garlic, chopped
1/4 cup lemon juice
3 tablespoons shallots, minced
2 teaspoons mixed dried herbs—equal parts of basil, oregano, thyme
2 tablespoons salt
1 cup sundried tomatoes, julienned
2 cups mushrooms, quartered
6 oz. Parmesan cheese, grated
1 cup roma tomatoes, seeded and julienned
1 bunch green onions, chopped
1 cup spinach, packed—washed and shredded into chiffonades
1 stick butter, cubed

1. Cook pastas until al dente—tender but still firm to bite.
2. Drain pasta thoroughly. Set aside.
3. Add white wine to hot sauté skillet and cook over high heat until half the wine evaporates.
4. Add olive oil, garlic, lemon juice, shallots, herbs and salt, sundried tomatoes, mushrooms, Parmesan cheese, and all the seafood to the skillet. Sauté on high heat until hot all the way through. Approximately 3–4 minutes.
5. Add pasta and heat thoroughly.
6. Finish by tossing in roma tomatoes, green onions, chopped spinach and butter. Cook until butter has melted into the sauce.
7. Serve hot with more Parmesan cheese sprinkled on top.
   *See Smoking section.

The
smoky
fruits of
the sea become
happy plate-mates with
the pasta, vino, and herbs.

THINGS WITH WINGS

Sometimes you don't know if you've gone too far until you've gone too far.

Duck Breast with Red Chili Glaze

Grilled Ostrich with Warm Strawberry Raspberry Sauce

Chili Stuffed Quail with Chipotle Cream

Chicken Nogales

Pheasant with Pesto

Wild Turkey with Corn Bread and Chorizo-Liver Pâté Stuffing and Harvest Cider Sauce

Smoked Goose Breast Stuffed with Apples and Onions Painted with Cinnamon Ancho Honey Sauce

Duck Breast

with Red Chili Glaze

Serves 8

Glaze and amaze! A glaze is a light brushed-on sauce. We feel that the best glazes are ones that have both a savory and a sweet side. In this recipe the smoke from the grill combines with the salty soy, the tart vinegar, and the sweet brown sugar for an amazing taste treat.

You can now buy ready-to-cook duck breast at butcher counters in good grocery stores. This is much easier than trying to de-bone the whole bird. All farm-raised duck has a layer of fat between the skin and the meat. When properly grilled over a hardwood fire the fat will be cooked away and the skin will be crisp.

A chef should imitate a duck—calm and unruffled on the surface, and paddling like crazy underneath.

"Shake a Tail Feather" —Ray Charles

VARIATIONS: The glaze is also great with chicken, pork, quail, and other game birds.

TIMING: Glaze can easily be made a day or two in advance.

Duck Breast

8 duck breasts (1 per person)
Red Chili Glaze

1. Score the skin and fat layer of the raw bird with a sharp knife in a crosshatch pattern.
2. Lightly season with salt and pepper.
3. Place the duck breast, skin side down, over a hot charcoal or hardwood fire. Keep a watchful eye as the duck fat will begin to cook out and the fire will flare up. If this happens, move the breast to the side until it dies down. Flame-kissed duck skin will become crispy and delicious.
4. Cook the breast skin-side down for the majority of the grill time—approximately 8 minutes depending on the heat of the fire. Turn breast over and grill the inside for 2 minutes maximum. You'll find that most good restaurants serve duck medium rare to medium, so don't be afraid of a little pinkness on the inside.
5. Slice the duck breast and fan it out on the plate to increase the eye appeal.
6. Serve topped with Red Chili Glaze.

TOOLS:
Grill
Heavy Saucepan
Chef's Knife
Whisk
Long Tongs

Red Chili Glaze

1 cup champagne vinegar
1 to 1 1/2 tablespoons red chili flakes (if you like it hot use 1 1/2 to 2 tablespoons flakes; if not, use 1 tablespoon or less)
1 tablespoon garlic, minced
2 tablespoons onions, minced
2 cups light brown sugar, packed
2 tablespoons tomato paste
1/2 cup soy sauce
1 teaspoon salt
1 stick sweet butter, cut into 8–10 chunks

1. Simmer champagne vinegar, chili flakes, garlic and onion in a heavy saucepan until reduced by half.
2. Add brown sugar, tomato paste, soy sauce and salt and bring back to a simmer for 3 minutes.
3. Remove from heat and whisk in butter chunks. This glaze can burn easily, so brush it on just prior to serving.

The hint of bitterness that comes off the grill is offset by the sweetness of the glaze.

Grilled Ostrich

with Warm Strawberry Raspberry Sauce
Serves 6

Because the ostrich doesn't fly, the meat on the breast is pretty much non-existent. However, because they can run upwards of 35–40 mph, they have some mighty big drumsticks!

Ostrich is extraordinarily lean and lends itself well to low, slow grilling. Because of the low fat content, your margin of error is diminished, so we suggest not cooking beyond medium, to insure a moist and juicy cut.

Things do not always taste as they appear.

"Love Me Tender" —Elvis Presley

VARIATION:	TIMING:	TOOLS:
Emu	Sauce can be made a day ahead of time and warmed to a simmer before serving.	Grill Blender Heavy Saucepan Food Processor Long Tongs

Grilled Ostrich

2 lb. ostrich steak (will feed approximately 6 people)

Have your butcher remove the connective tissue (silverskin) from the meat. Use the thick portions for grilling. Remember that ostrich is one of the leanest meats available, so it will dry out and be tough if over cooked.

Season your ostrich cut with salt and pepper. Turn it 4 times over medium high coals to mark it, about 30 seconds on each side. Move the ostrich away from direct heat and slowly cook to medium rare to medium. This should take 12–15 minutes. Turn it every 4–5 minutes.

After grilling, let the steak stand at room temperature for 3–4 minutes to allow the natural juices to return to the protein strands. Slice into 1/8" thick slices and fan out across warm Strawberry Raspberry Sauce and serve. Garnish with fresh berries.

Strawberry Raspberry Sauce*

1 pint strawberries, hulled
1 pint raspberries
1/4 cup raspberry vinegar
juice of 1 lemon
1/2 cup chardonnay or other white wine
1 stick sweet butter
1 tablespoon shallots or red onion, minced
1 tablespoon garlic, minced
3/4 cup granulated white sugar
1 teaspoon salt

1. In a blender, purée strawberries with raspberries, raspberry vinegar and lemon juice. Set aside.
2. Pour wine into a heavy-bottomed saucepan. Bring to a boil and reduce to just a couple of tablespoons.
3. Add butter, shallots, and garlic and lightly sauté until softened and clear.
4. Add sugar and salt and simmer two minutes.
5. Mix in the puréed fruits and heat through.
6. Adjust salt and pepper level and serve under grilled and sliced ostrich. Garnish with fresh berries.

*See Resources section.

The rich steak flavor of the bird combined with the rustic taste of the grill is set off by the tart berry sauce.

Chili Stuffed Quail

with Chipotle Cream
Serves 6

We created this recipe one year during the annual celebration of the arrival of the Hatch chilies from Hatch, New Mexico. For us it's like the new Beaujolais, the grunion running, or any other seasonal happening that provides an excuse for celebration and good eating.

The Hatch chilies are wonderful green chilies, milder than Anaheims, that symbolize the end of the summer. Somewhere between the end of August and the beginning of October, you can drive down Barton Springs Road in Austin, Texas and smell the smoke from peppers roasting in huge cages. Look for the Big Chili Roaster in front of Chuy's Restaurant—Home of Comida Deluxe! That's when we know the Hatch is officially in season.

We enjoy these chilies for their robust, big flavor and not-so-spicy burn. They are also sold frozen and in cans as New Mexico chilies. Some people use them in sauces, some in salsas and others on the tops of their hamburgers—but, of course, *we* like to stuff quail with them.

Four big chilies after charring, skinning, seeding, and chopping will yield a bit over 1 cup. Go ahead and put it all in. The red bell pepper provides a nice color balance, the reduced lime juice—tartness, and the finely diced tortillas soak up all the juices! The brown sugar and sweet corn round out the big chili flavor.

We always suggest the semi-boneless quail—easy to prepare and the easiest to eat! These should be available from any specialty food store but speak with your butcher about advance ordering. *(See Resources section.)*

The arrival of Hatch green chilies means the heat of summer is almost over—time to celebrate.

"Chili Today, Hot Tamale" —Ramsey Lewis

VARIATION:
Try this stuffing with a Cornish game hen.

TOOLS:
Blow Torch
Oven-proof Sauté Pan
Heavy-bottomed
    Saucepan
Blender

TIMING:
Quail can be stuffed in the morning for the evening meal.

Chili Stuffed Quail

4 Hatch green chilies, large
1 red bell pepper
3 tablespoons garlic, minced
3 tablespoons red onion, diced fine
6 tablespoons olive oil
1/4 cup lime juice
1 cup kernel corn
1 1/2 tablespoons brown sugar
1 1/2 teaspoons salt
4 corn tortillas, 1/4" dice
6 quail, semi-boneless
Chipotle Cream Sauce

Earthy roasted green chili pepper with tart lime juice and cilantro stuffed into a roasted quail . . . You know you're in Austin in the fall.

1. Roast, peel and seed Hatch chilies and red bell pepper *(see Pepper section)*. Dice and set aside.
2. Sauté garlic and onion in 2 tablespoons hot oil. Add lime juice and reduce until dry.
3. Add Hatch chilies, corn, red bell pepper, brown sugar, salt, and tortillas. Cool.
4. Stuff into boneless quail.
5. Sear stuffed quail on both sides, in a hot sauté pan with the rest of the olive oil.
6. Transfer to a 350° oven and roast for 12–15 minutes.
7. Serve with Chipotle Cream Sauce.

Chipotle Cream Sauce

2 cups chicken stock
3 cloves garlic, minced
3 shallots, chopped
1/4 cup sundried tomatoes
2 chipotle chilies
1 tablespoon Worcestershire sauce
4 dashes Tabasco®
1/4 cup brown sugar
1 teaspoon salt
1/2 cup cream
1 bunch cilantro, rough cut, leaves only

1. Combine all ingredients in a small saucepan except the cilantro and cream. Bring to a boil and simmer until chilies and tomatoes are softened.
2. Transfer to a blender and carefully purée. This mixture is very hot. Fill blender only half full at any one time.
3. Return to the pot and add cream and cilantro. Mix well.
4. Heat through and adjust seasonings.

Pheasant with Pesto

Serves 4

This is one of our new favorite summertime entrées at the restaurant. It combines the freshness of basil from our herb garden and the lightness of grilled pheasant. We grow more basil than anything else in our garden, even our neighboring Italian restaurant draws on our supply.

For instant aromatherapy, hold your head over the blender while making pesto and inhale deeply. You will achieve calm and be at cosmic oneness with the universe.

"I've Got You Under My Skin"
— Frank Sinatra

VARIATION: If pheasant is unavailable at your market, chicken is a great substitute. A 6-oz. boneless breast with skin on will be fine.

TIMING: The pheasant and the pesto are best made the day before. What the heck, go ahead and stuff it as well. Start the grill at least one hour before cooking to let the temperature reduce to a medium heat.

TOOLS:
Pastry Bag
Blender
Grill

Pheasant with Pesto

1/2 cup pine nuts
3 teaspoons garlic, minced
3/4 cup olive oil
2 cups basil leaves, packed tightly
2 tablespoons Parmesan cheese
1 1/2 teaspoons salt
2 pheasant (Ask your butcher to bone and halve the birds. Keep the bones to make stock later.)

1. Lightly toast pine nuts in a a dry skillet, stirring constantly until lightly browned. Let cool.
2. Begin making your Pesto. Combine pine nuts, garlic and oil in a blender and purée. Add basil and cheese and blend to a paste. Add salt to taste and set aside.
3. Take the boned pheasant (2 halves per bird) and gently loosen the skin from the meat with your fingers to create a pocket.
4. Place room-temperature pesto into a pastry bag with a wide tip. Pipe or squirt the pesto under the skin. Manipulate it with your fingers to evenly distribute it across the pheasant.
5. Begin grilling over medium heat, skin-side down and finish cooking skin-side up. This method will crisp the skin. Finishing skin-side up will allow the oil from the pesto to baste the bird. Total cooking time for the pheasant halves should be 13–15 minutes over a medium fire.

The basil pesto, with its minty Italian richness, tames the wild flavor of grilled game bird.

Smoked Goose Breast
Stuffed with Apples and Onions

Painted with Cinnamon Ancho Honey Sauce

Serves 6

This recipe always appears on our menu during the month of December. The Christmas season and smoked goose just seem to go together. Any hunter can tell you why—it's goose season in Texas.

As a teenager Jeff would go goose hunting west of Houston at Eagle Lake, the "Goose Capital of the World." He once brought home geese that had been eating fish. There was *nothing* that would make that meat tasty. The only use he found for it was cat food—they loved it.

In fact, the apples and onions in this recipe are an old hunter's trick to draw any strong game flavors from the meat. They were usually stuffed into the whole goose cavity and discarded after cooking. Farmed-raised geese have a mild pleasant taste, so the apples and onions are more for

tradition, and to add moisture and flavor.

Years ago we began experimenting with different flavors of smoke. Like any poultry or fowl, the goose absorbs the flavors from the smoke very quickly. Our first Christmas goose was smoked with a base of pecan wood coals smothered with grapevine from Fall Creek Vineyards and orange pekoe tea—what a wonderful spiced flavor.

Other memorable smoking combinations have included herbs picked from the garden just before the winter cold kills them. Basil is our favorite. A bowl of simmering wine or beer adds flavor and moisture, and crushed juniper berries collected from hill country cedars create a unique taste, as well. Use your imagination and create your own smoking accents.

VARIATION: If you have trouble locating goose breasts, this work very well with duck breast.

TIMING: We suggest you stuff the goose breast the morning of the meal, or 6–8 hours ahead of time. This way the stuffing doubles as a marinade.

"No diet will remove all the fat from your body because the brain is entirely fat. Without a brain you might look good, but all you could do is run for public office"
—Covert Bailey, diet and exercise guru

Chantilly Lace . . . "make you feel real loose like a long necked goose"
—the Big Bopper

TOOLS:

Smoker (see Smoking section)

Mandoline

Boning Knife

Zester

Blender

Squirt Bottle

Chef's Thermometer

Heavy-bottomed Stock Pot

Mesh Sieve

Smoked Goose Breast

6 goose breasts with skin-on
2 Red Delicious apples, cored and thinly sliced
2 Granny Smith apples, cored and thinly sliced
1 large yellow onion, peeled and thinly sliced } all on a mandoline
2 garlic cloves, mashed
3 tablespoons sugar
juice and zest of 2 oranges

1. Using a sharp boning knife, separate the skin from the breast to form a pocket. The knife can be used to start the pocket and your index finger to finish the job.
2. Combine all of the above ingredients (except the goose) in a bowl and toss. Then over-stuff each goose breast pocket.

3. If the goose is the farm-raised variety, you may want to score the outside of the skin with a series of "x"s to allow the fat to cook off while you are smoking.

4. Start a small wood or coal fire to one side of your smoker. Allow it to burn down to embers. Add your smoking medium and then the goose breast, away from the direct heat. Smoking close to 200–225° is ideal.

5. Smoke covered for 45 minutes, then check the internal temperature with a chef's thermometer. Make your heat adjustments at that point. Remember you do not want to cook the goose breast past an internal temperature of 160°.

6. Bring the goose inside and allow it to stand at room temperature for 5 minutes before slicing. Fan out on a plate. Get ready to paint with Cinnamon Ancho Honey.

Cinnamon Ancho Honey

5 ancho chilies
2 cups honey
2 tablespoons garlic, chopped
2 sticks cinnamon
2 tablespoons shallots, chopped
2 tablespoons chili powder
1 teaspoon cumin
1 tablespoon cocoa powder
1 teaspoon salt
1/4 cup water

1. Remove stems, seed pods and seeds from anchos and soak until softened in a 1/4 cup of water. Drain.

2. Combine honey, garlic, anchos, cinnamon, and shallots in a heavy bottomed sauce pot. Bring to a boil, remove from heat and let sit for 15 minutes.

3. Remove cinnamon sticks and discard. Transfer mixture to a blender and process until smooth.

4. Add chili powder, cumin, and cocoa with blender running. Taste and adjust seasoning with salt.

5. Strain through mesh sieve and pour into squirt bottles. Cool to room temperature and express yourself gloriously atop the goose.

Crisp apples, onion, and orange zest smoked into rich goose breast makes my mouth water.

MEATS
WILD AND TAME

We love animals. They're delicious.

Introduction—It's Mainly Because of the Meat

Protein Rules. When in doubt buy the bigger steak.

Kangaroo doesn't taste like chicken.

et's face it. Hudson's on the Bend is known for its wide variety of meats —wild and tame. The Texas Hill Country has been hunting territory for a long time and hunters here are serious about the sport. They are equally serious about eating the fruits of their labor. Frequently we are approached for information about how to dress and prepare wild game for the table.

Our reputation has gotten to the point that, when a kangaroo escaped from the zoo, a pair of local DJs kiddingly said they better come and find it quick before the boys from Hudson's got it and put it on the menu. We trotted over with some rattlesnake cakes and some wild boar. We made those boys eat their words.

Actually, kangaroo is the only marsupial we've ever cooked. And no, it doesn't taste like chicken. We have cooked antelope, caribou, deer, elk, moose, and just about every kind of split-hoofed horned animal. We even tried zebra once.

When we heard about a man in Wisconsin who was raising African lions, we naturally had to try it. The meat was pink and very sinewy and didn't go over well. Then we tried offering a Biblical special—lion and lamb lying down on the same plate, and it sold much better.

Once in Oklahoma, Jay made beaver chili. He says it tastes like armadillo, which tastes a little like ham roast, except more tender. Jay doesn't draw the line anywhere and is not particularly sentimental—Bambi, Rudolph, Thumper; the only lump in his throat for critters is when he's eating them. He has been known to complain that you "just can't get good squirrel any more."

Generally, Jay avoids brains (take that any way you want), but not necessarily heads. In Mexico they serve barbecoa, in which they remove the brains from a whole cow's head, roast it in the oven, then peel the meat off of the skull.

A friend of Jeff's in Colorado once shot a bear and brought home the steaks. Well, Jeff's reputation was on the line. He couldn't admit that he didn't have a recipe for bear.

Jeff decided to cook it in a big covered casserole. It turns out that bear is quite fatty, so he had to pour off fat three times. Rest assured, he won't get caught without a recipe again. I know he has one for elephant.

If you have had a bad game experience, it is most likely that the meat was not handled, butchered, dressed, or stored properly. If Uncle Fred strapped a deer onto his car and drove 12 hours back from deer camp through traffic; it may not have enhanced the flavor of the meat.

The big variable in the taste of game is what the animal has been grazing on.

The big variable in the taste of game is what the animal has been grazing on. Nowadays, most game is ranch raised, so their diet is controlled. The standard fare is natural grasses supplemented with corn or sorghum. This means you are unlikely to get any nasty surprises—like fish-eating geese.

Most game today has a mild, pleasant taste. The meat is lean and, if you are the least bit adventurous, there are plenty of new things to try.

Jef

Watermelon-Injected Pork Tenderloin

with Watermelon Salsa
Serves 6

This recipe screams late summertime when the watermelons are plentiful. It's for one of those evenings when you don't want to go inside and you're feeling just a little hungry. Barefoot children will soon be chasing fireflies and it's a fine night for grilling.

We originally came up with this recipe for ribs, but it proved to be wonderful for pork tenderloin. We use an injector, or syringe, to infiltrate the muscle fiber with the marinade (an injector or food syringe can be found in specialty food stores). Reserve a little marinade for basting.

You'll see that we use Midori liqueur (a Japanese liqueur with a honeydew flavor). It does give a delicate boost to the marinade, but buy a small bottle as it doesn't go with everything.

"When one has tasted watermelons, one knows what angels eat. It was not a southern watermelon that Eve took; we know it because she repented." –Mark Twain

"Watermelon Man" —Herbie Hancock

VARIATIONS: If you don't have an injector, just marinate tenderloin overnight. This marinade will also improve the taste of lesser cuts of meat, such as London Broil or chicken.

TIMING: For best results inject the meat the day before and store in an airtight plastic bag with extra marinade.

TOOLS:
Blender
Sieve or Strainer
Airtight Plastic Bags
Injector for Marinade
Grill

Marinade

3 cups diced watermelon meat
    (approximately, to yield 2 cups juice)
3 jalapeños (leave jalapeño ribs and
    seeds in for max heat, out for less)
1 tablespoon salt
2 cups granulated sugar
1/4 cup Midori liqueur (optional)
2 lbs. pork tenderloin
salt and pepper

1. Seed, then purée watermelon and jalapeños in a blender.
2. Strain mixture through a sieve and return to the blender. If you won't be injecting the tenderloin, don't worry about straining the marinade.
3. Add salt, sugar and Midori liqueur and blend for 2 minutes.
4. Reserve 1 cup for basting.
5. Draw marinade up into syringe-type injector. Poke and inject marinade throughout tenderloin.
6. After marinating, season the meat with some salt and pepper.
7. Have your coals prepared on the grill and use the combination technique of direct and indirect heat. Roll the tenderloin over the direct heat to establish some sexy grill marks and then move to a slower part of the grill to finish cooking.
8. Baste the tenderloin periodically throughout the cooking process.

Finishing over indirect heat will allow it to cook without burning.
9. Cook the tenderloin to an internal temperature of 145°. (Despite all the warnings from your mother about the need to cook pork to 170°, the truth is 137° will kill off anything that might harm you.) Allow the meat 5 minutes to rest, then slice into medallions. Fan across some Watermelon Salsa for a great summer meal.

Watermelon Salsa

2 cups watermelon, seeded and diced
    fine
1 Granny Smith apple, diced fine
1 red onion, julienned
2 cloves garlic, minced
1 mango, peeled and diced
2 jalapeños, seeded and diced fine
1 bunch cilantro, leaves only
2 tablespoons sugar
Salt and pepper to taste
2 limes, juice only
splash of rice wine vinegar

Combine all ingredients and chill well.

The crisp cool ...sh of
the watermelon ...sa
makes a re...ng
bed for th... and
sweet grilled
pork tenderloin.

Rib Eye Steak

in a Bock Beer Marinade
Serves 4–6

When Jay was just a young cook arriving in Texas from Oklahoma, the culinary rage was fajitas. Back then folks were marinating them in all sorts of stuff, and dark beer seemed to be in all the recipes. The brew was usually Heineken or some other German Dark. Shiner Bock had the reputation, at the time, as a cheapo beer, the bottom of the barrel dregs that could be had for a song, and with its inexpensive price it probably inspired a few.

Now, some 20 years later, thanks to pride and some fine regional ingredients, Shiner has become the prince of commercially-produced dark beers. Marinated and grilled beef is traditional in central Texas and we use big rib eye steaks with our Shiner Bock marinade. (It will work well with fajitas, too.)

The rib eye is our favorite and the most flavorful cut of beef. This is the same cut as prime rib but is the steak version, not the big roast. It comes from the forequarter of the animal between the 7th and 13th ribs. These steaks are characterized by an eye of fat in the center. The marbling is quite visible and is a prime factor in making a juicy and flavorful steak.

VARIATIONS: This is also a wonderful marinade for baby-back ribs, portabello mushrooms, chicken . . . you get the idea.

TIMING: Marinate the steaks in an airtight plastic bag the day before grilling to achieve the optimum flavor.

TOOLS:
Grill or Broiler
Large Airtight Plastic Bags

"God sends meat, the devil sends the cook." —Thomas Deloney

Rib Eye Steak

6 rib eye steaks

We use 14–16 oz. rib eyes at Hudson's and even though it's a lot of steak, the plates always come back clean.

Shiner Bock Marinade

1 12-oz. Shiner Bock, or your local or homemade dark beer
2 tablespoons garlic, chopped
2 tablespoons red onion, diced fine
2 tablespoons Worcestershire sauce
4 shakes Tabasco®
Juice of 2 limes
1/4 cup brown sugar, packed
1 tablespoon coarse brown mustard (Creole is good)
2 tablespoons olive oil
2 teaspoons salt

1. Combine all ingredients except salt. Salt in the marinade draws too much moisture from the meat over an extended time.
2. Pour over steaks and marinate from 4 hours to overnight.
3. Cook the steaks over medium-high heat about 4 minutes each side for medium rare to medium. (See "In Your Face Grilling.")
4. Season with salt to taste after cooking.

"Beer Barrel Polka" —Lawrence Welk

The natural sweetness of the beer with the other savory ingredients pairs well with beef, especially when cooked on the grill.

Elk or Caribou Backstrap
Stuffed with Chorizo
in Mango Jalapeño Sauce

Serves 6–8

This recipe is simply delicious and while it sounds exotic, it's deliciously simple. It began with pork tenderloin over ten years ago. In fact you'll still see it featured on "Great Chefs of the West" which always seems to be running on PBS or the Discovery channel somewhere. Over the years we have gotten creative and experimented with every kind of split-hoofed, horned animal. All can be delicious, but it works ideally with elk or caribou.

At Christmas we put reindeer, the domesticated version of caribou, on the menu. We call it the Rudolph Special and, having no shame, sometimes serve it with a maraschino cherry.

Chorizo is a Mexican sausage—coarsely ground fresh pork, seasoned with garlic and chilies. Talk to your local butcher or meat manager for a Mexican-influenced sausage from your area. We also have used the wild game filling for our enchiladas as the stuffing for this recipe.

"You better not pout, you better not cry."

Theme from "Northern Exposure"

VARIATION: The original pork tenderloin version is well worth tasting. Figure 6 ounces per person.

TOOLS:
Food Processor
Skillet and Saucepan
Grill
Boning Knife

TIMING: You can prepare the chorizo stuffing 2–3 days ahead and stuff the tenderloin a day ahead, if you like.

Elk or Caribou Backstrap

4 lbs. boneless backstrap of elk
1 lb. of chorizo or Wild Game Enchilada Stuffing, chilled
6 tablespoons Bronze Rub *(see Salt and Seasoning section)*
2 cups Mango Jalapeño Sauce

1. Trim away any silverskin from the elk backstrap.
2. Cut backstrap into 6 elongated pieces with the grain of the meat.
3. Insert a fillet, or boning, knife into the center of each piece lengthwise and pierce through.
4. Using your fingers, open up the pocket from both ends, and gently expand it.
5. Overstuff pocket as much as possible with the chorizo stuffing, without blowing out the sides. If the side does tear, that's okay, just be sure to slice backstrap tear-side down after grilling.
6. Season elk loin with Bronze Rub and cook over medium-hot coals for about 10–12 minutes, turning the meat every 2–3 minutes, until it reaches an internal temperature of 130°.
7. Slice into medallions and fan over warmed Hudson's Mango Jalapeño sauce.

Chorizo or Wild Game Enchilada Stuffing

1 large yellow onion, minced
1 large carrot, minced
6 cloves garlic, minced
1–2 jalapeños, minced *(for extra spicy, leave the seeds and ribs in)*
3 ribs celery, minced
1 lb. chorizo or wild game (beef and pork mix, game birds, chicken, or any combination of the above to total 1 lb.)
2 tablespoons dark chili powder
2 tablespoons ground cumin
1 tablespoon (or more) salt

The spicy south of the border sausage surrounded by the wild game of the north is enough to make Dudley Do-Right run off with Dorothy Lamour.

1. Mince onion, carrot, garlic, and jalapeño in a processor with an S-blade. Half full is about right. Never overload your food processor. Rough chop veggies first; make sure you have a sharp blade.
2. Hand chop the celery, as it gets stringy if you try to chop it in the processor.
3. If using chorizo, remove casings, crumble and cook in a sauté pan until lightly browned. Drain off all excess fat. Or, if using wild game or other meats, grind the meat in a food processor fitted with an S-blade, or mince with a sharp knife. Brown meat until almost all the fat is rendered.
4. Add veggies and spices to sauté pan. These vegetables provide a depth of flavor and moisture to the very lean elk or caribou.
5. Simmer 20 minutes and set aside to cool completely before stuffing the backstrap.

Mango Jalapeño Sauce (the Fearless way)

1 lb. mangoes, peeled and diced
1 1/2 cups granulated sugar
3 tablespoons champagne vinegar
2 tablespoons garlic, chopped
3 tablespoons red onion, diced
4 jalapeños, seeded and sliced
1 teaspoon salt

1. Combine mangoes, sugar, vinegar, garlic, and red onion. Bring to a boil.
2. Reduce to a simmer and cook 10 minutes.
3. Add jalapeños and season with salt.

Antlers and Claws: the Austin-Boston Combo

Venison Backstrap Stuffed with Smoked Lobster in a Guava Sour Cherry Sauce

Serves 8–10

This was Jay's first hint of the drift to *No Fear Combinations*. About ten years ago, Jeff was looking around for a new way to put together some on-hand ingredients. Yes, at Hudson's venison backstrap and smoked lobster are "on-hand" ingredients.

When he proposed this unique combination, Jay thought it was kind of off-the-wall; and then Jeff added the guava sour cherry sauce and Jay suspected that he had really gone too far this time. But the king of "there's no such thing as too much" had just found a new way of hitting on those major tastebud groups. This has since become a signature item—one of the restaurant's most requested dishes. Anyone can serve Surf and Turf, but only Hudson's has Antlers and Claws.

Stuffing . . . not just for Thanksgiving anymore! A way of life at Hudson's.

"Hunter Gets Captured by the Game"
—Jerry Garcia

VARIATIONS: Any game or exotic backstrap would do . . . elk, caribou, fallow, antelope, even beef tenderloin would be great.

TIMING: Smoke the lobster a day ahead and prep the backstrap several hours before cooking.

Antlers and Claws: the Austin-Boston Combo

4 lbs. boneless backstrap of venison *(see Resources section)*
2 lbs. lobster tail meat, smoked *(see Smoking section)*

1. Cut backstrap into 4"–5" long portions, or get your butcher to do it.
2. Using a fillet knife, pierce the end, sliding the boning knife lengthwise until it appears at the other end of the backstrap and makes a pocket. Stick your fingers in from both ends and gently open and expand the pocket.
3. Cut smoked lobster into 1" cubes. Stuff into backstrap from both ends until it's ready to explode. If in doubt, overstuff! Refrigerate until time to grill.
4. Over medium-hot coals, cook the stuffed backstrap for 8–10 minutes, rotating every 2 minutes.
5. Warm Guava Sour Cherry Sauce and pool on the plate.
6. Slice the backstrap and fan over sauce.

TOOLS:
Smoker
Grill or Broiler
Boning Knife
Chef's Knife or Scissors for Lobster Shell

Guava Sour Cherry Sauce

You always have the option of ordering a jar ready made—we won't tell. (See the Resources section.) But if you're in a fearless frame of mind, you can try making it from scratch. This sauce is great with pork, duck, or any game dish.

1 cup guava paste (6 oz. tin available in specialty stores)
1 cup dried sour cherries
2 tablespoons garlic, minced
2 tablespoons shallots, minced
1 cup frozen apple juice concentrate, thawed
1 cup water
1 cup brown sugar, packed
1 tablespoon salt, or to taste
1/2 cup raspberry vinegar

Combine all ingredients in a heavy saucepan and simmer over medium heat for 20 minutes.
Note: If you can't find guava paste, try 1 cup dried apricots stewed with 1/2 cup hot water and puréed in the blender.

Smoky briny lobster, rich backstrap of venison, the tartness of cherries and guava, and some sweetness to balance the sauce.

Sirloin of Beef in a Rosemary Crust

with Creole Mustard Sauce

Serves 8

Sirloin of Texas beef is one of our favorites for both flavor and texture. When wrapped and roasted in this rosemary crust, the beef stays moist and tender while taking on a wonderful herb flavor. Rosemary is one of the strongest, most pungent herbs and needs to be used with restraint to avoid being overpowering. But a sirloin of beef can stand up to the flavor and take full advantage of it.

"It's what's for dinner–Beef."
–American Beef Council

"Rawhide" —The Blues Brothers version

VARIATION: This recipe is also very tasty with a small beef tenderloin or venison. For a sauce, we recommend Hudson's on the Bend Mexican Marigold Mustard (see Resources section).

TIMING: Make the sauce a day ahead of time.

TOOLS:
Flat Dishes for Breading
Heavy Bottomed Skillet
Food Processor with S-Blade
Saucepan

Rosemary Crust

1 1/2 cup fresh rosemary, cleaned from stem
1 cup pine nuts
2 cups dry bread crumbs
1/2 cup garlic, minced
1/2 cup shallots, minced
2 tablespoons salt

1. Toast pine nuts in a dry skillet, stirring constantly until lightly browned.
2. Combine all ingredients in food processor with S-blade. Pulse to a coarse texture.
3. Pour into flat dish to coat steak.

Seasoned Egg Wash

1/3 cup Hudson's on the Bend Mustard or your favorite spicy mustard
1/4 cup green peppercorns, drained (they come in a tin or a jar)
8 egg yolks
1/4 cup milk

1. Combine all ingredients in a food processor and blend until the peppercorns are minced.
2. Put in dish to dip steaks.

Sirloin of Beef

8 12-oz. sirloin steaks
1 cup all-purpose flour
1/2 cup olive oil for sautéing
Seasoned Egg Wash
Rosemary Crust
Creole Mustard Sauce

1. Trim all the fat off the sirloin. It's color-coded—throw away the white and keep the red.
2. Sear each side of the sirloin in a very hot skillet.
3. After searing, chill sirloin in refrigerator before breading.
4. Dust sirloin with flour and dip in seasoned egg wash. Roll and press in the crust mixture, coating the entire sirloin.
5. Heat a large skillet with 1/2 cup olive oil until approximately 325°. A rosemary leaf will pop when it touches the oil. Sauté each steak (2 or 3 at a time) until browned on both sides—approximately 4 minutes on each side. If you want your sirloin cooked past rare–medium rare, pop it in a 350° oven another 3 minutes for medium, or 6 minutes for medium well.
6. Serve atop Creole Mustard Sauce.

The pungent rosemary is equalized by the tang of mustard sauce as rich sirloin flavor pops out.

Creole Mustard Sauce

2 tablespoons garlic, minced
2 tablespoons shallots, minced
1/2 cup red wine
1/2 cup rich veal stock
1/2 cup cream
1/2 cup Creole mustard
1 teaspoon salt
1 teaspoon cracked black pepper

1. Combine garlic, shallots and wine in a saucepan and simmer over medium-high heat until red wine has reduced to almost dry.
2. Add veal stock and cream, return to a boil.
3. Add Creole mustard, salt and cracked pepper. Simmer for two minutes and serve with sirloin.

Wild Boar Schnitzel

with Apple Cider Brandy Sauce

Serves 6

In the fall of 1989, the legendary Mimi Sheraton, former *New York Times* food critic, came to town. She was so famous that she had to use disguises when dining in New York restaurants. Some of the cagier ones had pictures of her posted in the kitchen to alert the staff.

Jeff once read an article that called her the "redoubtable Mimi." Not familiar with "redoubtable," he sidled over to Webster's and found, "One to be feared with a reverence" or "causing fear or alarm." Thank God we're fearless, but even better, we didn't know she was here.

Anyway, at the time, Mimi was working for Conde Nasts' *Traveler Magazine*. She loved our Hill Country cuisine, and was so smitten with our wild boar schnitzel that she awarded us a position on her list of the top 50 restaurants in the country.

The Texas Hill Country has a rich German heritage so schnitzel quite probably *is* the ancestor of Texas chicken fried steak. Schnitzel is German for "cutlet" which usually describes meat dipped in egg, breaded and fried—sound familiar?

Wild boar or feral hog, now hunted in the area, are formerly domesticated pigs. Their ancestors abandoned the "so-called" civilized world and escaped to the wild. These porcines bear little resemblance to their domesticated counterparts in temperament or size. Foraging for food keeps these guys lean and mean, with a distinct flavor that makes a fine schnitzel.

Apples and brandy go well with pork or boar. We've always served this schnitzel with apple cider brandy sauce, which later became so popular in its own right that we started selling it in jars. To make it simple, just open a jar of our Apple Cider Brandy Sauce, or make your own. Warm the sauce with julienned cuts of green apple for some great crunch.

Ich bin ein Bubba.

"Lichtensteiner Polka" —Will Glahe

VARIATION: You may use a smoked pork tenderloin instead of boar.

TIMING: Smoke boar and prepare bread crumbs 1 day ahead.

TOOLS:
Food Processor or Blender
Mallet
Skillet
Plastic Wrap
Smoker
Large Sauté Pan

Wild Boar Schnitzel

2 lbs. raw, boneless loin of boar (makes 6 medallions)
2 tablespoons Smoke Rub *(see Salt and Seasoning section)*
2 cups bread crumbs
2 eggs, beaten
1 cup milk
1 cup flour
1/2 cup clarified butter
Salt and pepper to taste
1 1/2 cups Hudson's Apple Cider Brandy Sauce*
1 Granny Smith apple, julienned

1. Season the loin with the Smoke Rub and smoke it 1 to 1 1/2 hours until medium rare to medium, an internal temperature of 140°. Slow smoking helps to tenderize and imparts a delicious flavor. Remove from smoker and refrigerate whole.

Big Flavors: Smoked boar, apples, brandy, and butter meet Big Textures: Crunchy apples, smooth sauce, and tender crust.

2. Grind dried bread crumbs in food processor. We use crumbs from our pumpkin bread, but a dried French loaf or sourdough is fine.

3. Slice loin into medallions 1/2" to 3/4" thick. Between plastic wrap, pound with a mallet to an even 1/4" thickness. Season the pounded medallions with salt and pepper.

4. Combine eggs and milk and beat to make egg wash. Pass seasoned medallion through flour, then egg wash and then bread crumbs.

5. Heat the clarified butter in a large sauté pan over medium high heat until shimmering (325°–350°).

6. Carefully lay in 3 cutlets and cook 1 1/2 to 2 minutes per side until the crust is set and golden. Turn and cook the other side for an additional 2 minutes. Remove from heat and hold warm. Repeat with remaining cutlets.

7. Combine Apple Cider Brandy Sauce and julienned apples in a saucepan and warm through. Spoon onto plate and top with schnitzel.

Apple Cider Brandy Sauce*

3/4 cup apple juice concentrate, thawed
1/2 cup water
2 tablespoons garlic, chopped
4 tablespoons red onion, diced
1/2 cup brown sugar, packed
1/2 cup brandy
1/2 teaspoon salt
1/4 teaspoon white pepper

1. Combine in a saucepan, bring to a boil, reduce to a simmer, and cook 10 minutes.

2. Adjust seasoning and serve hot under the schnitzel.

Or order through the Resources section.

Venison Stew

with Wild Mushrooms and Biscuits
Serves 6

Attention all you hunters who have been putting away venison in the freezer. Here's your chance to take some of those less-than-tender cuts and make a wonderful meal.

The key to this recipe is the use of a rich veal stock or venison stock enhanced with the earthly delight of porcini mushrooms reduced with a large amount of red wine. The pieces of venison are seared to bring out the flavor and it's all topped off with homemade biscuits.

Thinking about it, this is another version of Shepherd's Pie, using biscuits instead of mashed potato. This dish is hearty fare well suited for the few cold nights we have here in Austin. Be sure to make extra biscuits!

**"In the end everything is stew." –
Molly O'Neill**

"Get your biscuits in the oven and your buns in the bed"
—Kinky Friedman

VARIATION: To make your own version you could vary the mushrooms—shiitake or portobello instead of porcinis.

TIMING: Stew can be made a day ahead and reheated before topping with biscuits for the oven.

TOOLS:
Sauce Pot, Cast Iron Pot, Rolling Pin, Chef's Knife, Biscuit Cutter, Mixing Bowl, Cheese Grater

Venison Stew

1 lb. venison, fully trimmed 1" dice
1 cup flour with 3/4 tablespoon salt and 1 teaspoon white pepper added
1/2 cup clarified butter or olive oil
2 tablespoons garlic, chopped
2 tablespoons red onion, diced fine
2 cups burgundy (red) wine
4 oz. dried porcini mushrooms (Italian)
1 quart rich veal stock (see Stock Options)
2 small Idaho potatoes, medium dice
1 yellow onion, julienned
1 poblano pepper
2 ribs celery, diced fine
1 small carrot, julienned
1 red bell pepper, diced fine
2 dashes Tabasco®
1 1/2 tablespoons Worcestershire Sauce
1 1/2 tablespoons salt
1/2 teaspoon white pepper

1. Blister skin on poblano. Peel, seed and dice fine.
2. Heat butter or oil in a heavy bottomed pot until it just begins to smoke, about 350°.
3. Toss venison in seasoned flour, dusting off excess.
4. Add venison and brown in small batches. Reserve warm.
5. In the same pot, add garlic and red onion and sauté briefly. Add red wine and mushrooms, and reduce to one cup.
6. Add veal stock, potatoes, vegetables, and seasonings. Bring to a boil, reduce to a simmer and cook until potatoes are softened.
7. Add venison and adjust seasonings. Top pot with biscuits and bake in a preheated 450° oven for 10–12 minutes until biscuits are browned.

Buttermilk Biscuits

Makes about 24

3 cups sifted all-purpose flour
1 teaspoon salt
4 teaspoons double acting baking powder
2 teaspoons sugar
1 teaspoon baking soda
1 1/2 sticks unsalted butter, cut in 1/4" pieces
1 1/2 cups buttermilk
2/3 cup grated cheese, Monterey Jack and cheddar
1/4 cup green onion tops, chopped

1. Sift together dry ingredients.
2. Cut in the butter to the consistency of coarse cornmeal.
3. Make a well in the center of the dough and quickly incorporate buttermilk (about 30 seconds).
4. Knead gently on a floured board incorporating cheese and onions (about 30 seconds).
5. Pat out to 1 1/2" thickness and cut into large 4" biscuits. Set aside until step 7 above.

Earthy porcinis, rich venison stew, and piping hot biscuits.

Wild Game Chili

"The Official State Food of Texas"

Serves 10–12

"Next to jazz music, there is nothing that lifts the spirit and strengthens the soul more than a good bowl of chili."
–Harry James

It may be the official state food, but recipes and styles are as varied as the Texas landscape. After judging several of the larger chili cook-offs, we learned some of the unwritten rules of chili cooking etiquette: Never use beans of any kind. Drink 6 beers for every one that goes in the chili. And never use ground meat, it must be cubed.

Another thing we discovered is the strange phenomenon of *Secret Ingredient Syndrome*. After the winner is announced at a cook-off, the other serious chili chefs scramble to find out the winning ingredient and add it to *their* secret recipe. The result, after years of the same people going from contest to contest, is that the chili all looks and tastes remarkably similar. The more we judge these contests, the more sure we are of this.

The truth is that on a wet, cold Texas winter day nothin' tastes better than a bowl of "Texas Red." The following recipe is one that uses Texas venison and wild boar along with some of our favorite "secret" ingredients . . . good veal stock and ancho chilies!!!!

"Millie make some chili—make it burn, burn, burn."
—Billy Vera and the Beaters

VARIATION: Hunters, this is the recipe to clean out the wild game freezer. Use it all—elk, moose, bear, all kinds of antelope. We refrain from using game sausage, but if you must—you must. If game is not readily available, substitute some beef.

TIMING: The chili recipe can be made a day or two ahead of time . . . it just gets better in the refrigerator.

TOOLS:
8-Quart Heavy-bottom Stock Pot
Blender
Zester

Wild Game Chili

2 poblano chilies
6 ancho chilies
1/2 lb. bacon, ground
1 lb. venison, 1/4" cube (hindquarter is the best)
1 lb. wild boar, 1/4" cube (hindquarter is the best)
2 lbs. yellow onions, 1/4" dice
1/2 cup garlic, minced
2 ribs celery, diced
2 cups tomatoes, 1/4" dice
2 cups veal stock *(see Stock Options)*
juice and zest of 1 lemon
2 tablespoons brown sugar
3 tablespoons cumin
1/4 cup chili powder
2 tablespoons salt
2 teaspoons cayenne (diced jalapeño or serrano peppers are a great substitute for dry cayenne)

1. Blister skin from poblanos, peel, then remove seeds and ribs. Cut into 1/4" dice.
2. Remove seeds from ancho chilies. Soak in half cup water to soften about 10 minutes. Purée in blender with a little veal stock. Set aside.
3. Render the fat from the bacon and reserve the cooked bacon and the drippings.
4. Clean all the venison and wild boar free of connective tissue and silverskin, and with a sharp knife cube into 1/4" pieces.
5. Next, brown the meat in small batches using high heat, a large heavy pot or skillet and several tablespoons of bacon drippings. By cooking in small batches you will sear and brown the meat quickly. This will give you the proper texture and color—rich brown, not gray.
6. Remove the meat and set aside while you sauté the onions, garlic, celery, and poblanos in the same pot used for the meat. Add bacon drippings as needed.
7. Add the cooked bacon then the tomatoes, veal stock, lemon juice and zest, brown sugar, cumin, chili powder and puréed anchos.
8. Bring to a boil and reduce to a simmer. Add the browned meat and simmer slowly for 45 minutes to an hour, adding a little beer or water as it becomes too thick.
9. Toppings vary from salsa to grated cheese, goat cheese or flavored sour creams. We are partial to our Tomatillo White Chocolate Sauce as a topper.

Rich, earthy,
meaty, warm.

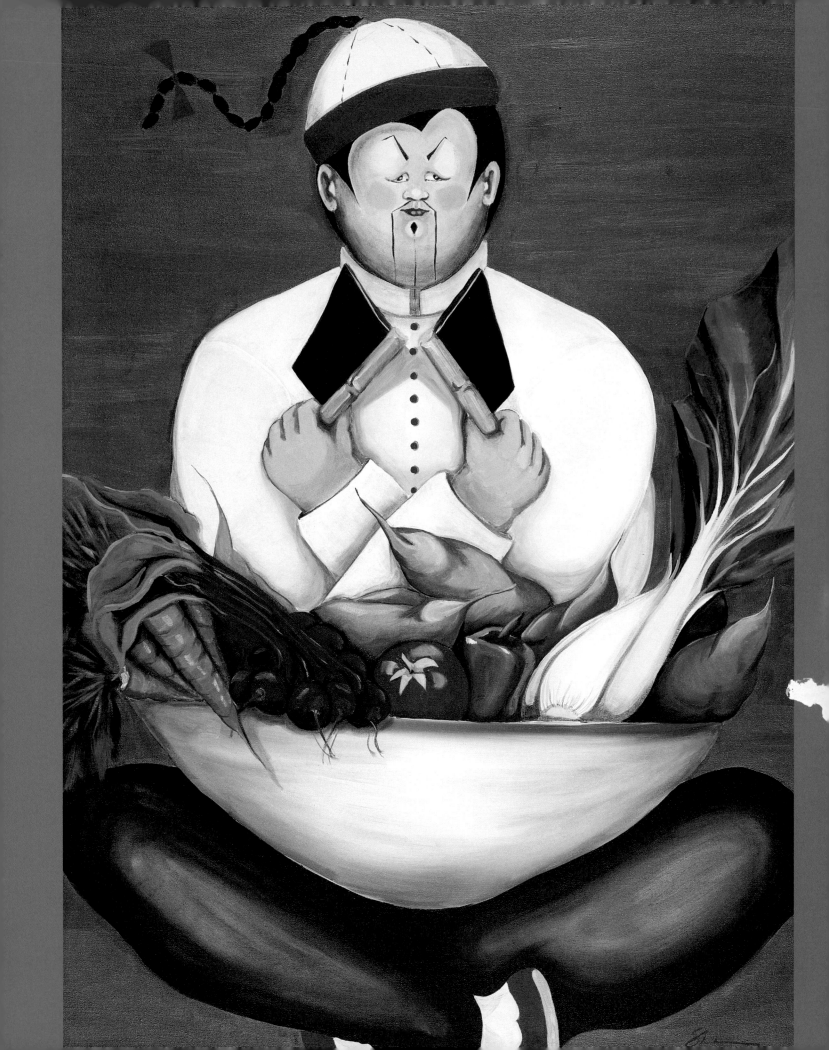

VEGETABLES AND SIDE DISHES

Cook what your mother taught you—but add 2 more jalapeños.

Eggplant Hudson's with Tomato Sauce

Jalapeño Stilton Blue Cheese Grits (Texas Polenta)

Corn Pudding . . . and Never Too Late Corn Cakes

Hudson's Nutmeg Scalloped Potatoes

Balsamic Asparagus

Ancho Bock Beer Smashers

Napa Cabbage

Hudson's Variable Veggies

Bourbon Vanilla Praline Sweet Potatoes

Eggplant Hudson's
with Tomato Sauce
Serves 6

To a certain extent, cooks are gypsies in white coats. Most of us, particularly when we're starting out, live like vagabonds, wandering from restaurant to restaurant—changing jobs about every 18 months to two years. Not lost, exploring!

It's a part of earning your membership in the community of chefs. We both did it. Along the way we had the chance to absorb new tastes, ingredients, and techniques. One day, if you're lucky, like we are, you settle in and the gypsies come to you. Each one brings something fresh to the mix so the menu keeps improving.

One such gypsy who sojourned at Hudson's was Joannie Crenshaw. She introduced us to this wonderful way with eggplant. (She then went on to become a doctor.) Here's to the gypsies past, present and future.

A side dish with so much attitude that it pushes the entrée right off the plate.

"Eggplant that Ate Chicago" —Dr. West's Medicine Show & Junk Band

---

VARIATION: Add 1/2 lb. crab meat as topping and voilà, it's an entrée.

TIMING: Once the eggplant is rolled up it can be refrigerated over night.

TOOLS: Food Processor, Mandoline, Chef's Knife, Sauté Pan

Eggplant Hudson's

1 eggplant 6–8" long
1 cup buttermilk
1 stick butter, melted
2 tablespoons Parmesan
1 bunch parsley, finely chopped for garnish

Seasoned Flour

2 cups flour
1 tablespoon oregano
1 tablespoon thyme
1 tablespoon basil
1 teaspoon salt
1/4 teaspoon white pepper

Filling

1 bunch cilantro, chopped
4 oz. goat cheese
1 cup ricotta
1 tablespoon shallots, minced
1 tablespoon garlic, minced
1/4 teaspoon salt
1/4 teaspoon white pepper
1 teaspoon oregano
1 teaspoon thyme
1 teaspoon basil
2 cups Hudson's Tomato Sauce (recipe follows)

1. Peel and, on mandoline, slice eggplant (the long way) into 12 1/8" slices
2. Mix flour, oregano, thyme, basil, 1 teaspoon salt and 1/4 teaspoon white pepper in a flat dish.
3. Pass eggplant slices through buttermilk. Dredge in seasoned flour.
4. Sauté briefly in half the butter, but do not brown.
5. Pat dry and set aside to cool.
6. To make filling, chop cilantro in the food processor and pulse in goat cheese, ricotta, shallots, garlic, 1/4 teaspoon salt, 1/4 teaspoon white pepper, and herbs.
7. Place 2 tablespoons of filling on one end of eggplant slice and roll up. The eggplant can be prepared to this point and refrigerated over night.
8. Sauté eggplant in remaining butter over medium heat until browned on all sides and hot in the center.
9. Pool 2 tablespoons of Hudson's Tomato Sauce on a plate, place two eggplant rolls on this, and top with more tomato sauce.
10. Garnish with Parmesan and chopped parsley.

Hudson's Tomato Sauce

2 tablespoons red onion, diced fine
3 garlic cloves, sliced
2 tablespoons olive oil
1/2 teaspoon leaf thyme, fresh
3 tablespoons tomato paste
Juice and zest of 1 lemon
3 tablespoons red wine
6 roma tomatoes, peeled, seeded, and chopped
1/4 cup fresh basil, chopped
1 teaspoon sugar
1 teaspoon kosher salt

1. Heat olive oil over medium-high heat. Add onion and garlic and sauté briefly.
2. Add thyme, tomato paste and lemon zest. Sauté for one minute.
3. Add wine and lemon juice and bring to boil.
4. Add tomatoes and bring back to a boil. Reduce heat and simmer until heated through. Toss in basil.
5. Adjust seasonings with sugar and kosher salt. The sugar cuts the acidity of the tomatoes.

The texture and flavor of the ricotta with the tantalizing crunch of the little crust. This is far too good to serve only to vegetarians.

Jalapeño Stilton Blue Cheese Grits

(Texas Polenta)
Serves 10–12

Jeff came up with this recipe for his parent's fiftieth wedding anniversary celebration. Since there were quite a few sophisticated septuagenarians on the guest list, some of whom had lived abroad, he wanted to do something elegant, yet with Hudson's style. Stilton, an English blue cheese with hefty character, plus down-home Texas grits creates a dish with Texas taste and international style.

In Texas we use dried pulverized hominy and call it grits. In Italy they use corn meal and call it polenta. In Mexico it's posole. At Café Beaujolais in Northern California, they tried putting grits on the menu and no one was interested. They changed the name to polenta and had a hit on their hands. In Santa Fe, New Mexico, posole (a hominy-enriched soup) is traditionally served on Thursdays in the style of a British high tea. Call it what you will, dress it up any way you want, it tastes good in any language. The ultimate cheese grits.

A mush by any other name would taste as sweet.

"If I don't love you baby, grits ain't grocery, eggs ain't poultry, and Mona Lisa was a man." "Grits Ain't Groceries" —Little Milton

VARIATION: Try different cheeses— Monterey Jack, smoky cheddar, Gouda, Edam, even Gorgonzola, though we do suggest you avoid Limburger. Nobody's that fearless. Or how about a little bacon?

TIMING: These grits are very sturdy and can hold at a warm 175° for 1–2 hours. Great for a buffet.

TOOLS:
12x12 Casserole
Whisk
Large Sauce Pot
Chef's Knife

Jalapeño Stilton Blue Cheese Grits

1 1/2 quarts water
1 stick of butter
1 cup red onion, diced
1/4 cup garlic
1 cup cream
2 jalapeños, diced
1 yellow bell pepper, diced
1 1/2 tablespoons salt
3 cups quick grits
8 eggs
1 lb. Stilton blue cheese

1. Remove stems, ribs and seeds from the yellow bell pepper and jalapeños. Leave ribs and seeds in jalapeños if you like the heat.
2. Bring water, butter, onion, garlic, cream, peppers, and salt to a simmer.
3. Add the grits and, stirring constantly, cook at a simmer for 3 minutes until soft and creamy.
4. Set aside to cool.
5. Whisk in beaten eggs and crumbled Stilton cheese. Mix well.
6. Grease a 12x12 casserole and dust with flour.
7. Pour in grit mixture and bake at 350° for 40–45 minutes or until firm.

The richness
of the corn
is balanced
by the sharp
cheese.

Corn Pudding . . .

and Never Too Late Corn Cakes

Serves 10–12

Dottie was so proud of her boy—cooking for George W. Bush!

Our corn pudding recipe is the restaurant's most requested recipe—bar none. We wish it was an original, but we cannot tell a lie. It has been Jeff's mother's holiday standby for as long as anyone can remember. She isn't sure where she found it, but thinks it came from one of those innumerable Junior League cookbooks.

At any rate, we have changed it so many times over the years, we suppose now it *is* more original than when we started. We like ours a little on the spicy side so we add cayenne and poblano peppers along with the sweet mild peppers.

Sometimes very creative things happen when the pressure is on. It was the end of a very busy night and a large group of regular customers came in just before closing. We were tired and not paying attention to how much corn pudding was left. Just before their entrees were to go out, we saw that we were out of corn pudding—and it takes 40 minutes to cook. What to do?!

That was the night the corn pudding pancakes were first made. We just ladled the batter onto a hot skillet with a little corn oil underneath. In 5 minutes they were ready to be served with the entrée.

Cook what your mother taught you—
but add 2 more jalapeños.

"Corn Shucking Party in Georgia"
—Herschel Brown

VARIATION: One of the beauties of this recipe is that it is so flexible and sturdy that you can modify it any number of ways without losing its personality. Change the peppers to sundried tomatoes, if you please. Add different herbs like fresh basil, Mexican Marigold Mint, whatever you like. Try dried mushrooms, like porcinis or shiitake.

TIMING: You can make the batter the day before and store it in a bowl in the refrigerator. Just give it a whisk before putting it in a greased and floured casserole dish at baking time. This recipe is so sturdy you can bake it early and hold it on warm or in a chafing dish.

TOOLS:
9x9 Casserole Dish
Mixing Bowls
Whisk or Whip
Chef's Knife

Dry Mix:

1 1/4 cups flour
1/3 cup granulated sugar
2 1/2 tablespoons baking powder
1/2 teaspoon salt
1/2 teaspoon cayenne pepper

Wet Mix:

6 whole eggs
1 stick of butter, melted
1/2 cup heavy cream
1 8-oz. can creamstyle corn

The sweetness and creaminess of the corn hides the surprise fire of the pepper.

Veggie Mix:

1 medium poblano pepper
1 medium red bell pepper
1 Anaheim pepper
1 lb. fresh cut corn

1. Pre-heat oven to 350°.
2. Combine all dry ingredients in a bowl. Mix well and set aside.
3. In a second bowl, whisk the eggs until blended, then add melted butter, cream, and cream style corn.
4. Blend the dry ingredients into the wet ingredients using a wire whisk.
5. Clean all three peppers, discarding the seeds and stems. Dice into 1/4" pieces.
6. Add fresh cut corn kernels and the diced peppers to the mixing bowl. Blend together.
7. Coat a medium-size casserole dish with butter or light vegetable oil and dust with flour.
8. Add the mix to the casserole dish. The depth can vary from 1 inch to 2 inches. If the mix is only 1 inch deep it will cook 5 to 10 minutes faster.
9. Place in a pre-heated oven at 350° and bake for 40 minutes or until it is golden brown and firm.

Hudson's Nutmeg
Scalloped Potatoes

Serves 12

In the early days of Hudson's there was a group of Germans who came over on tourist visas and ended up staying awhile. They loved nutmeg—nutmeg with venison, nutmeg with wild boar, nutmeg with pheasant. While they did get a little carried away at times, they taught us the power of nutmeg to conjure up feelings of warmth and good cheer. It made our kitchen smell like Christmas all the time.

One day they got loose in the potatoes, gave it the German treatment and took comfort food to the next great level, a gooey taste sensation. Thank you Riner, Elizbeth and Harold Katzenberger.

VARIATION: Leave the bacon out and call it vegetarian.

TIMING: Prepare in the morning for an evening meal.

TOOLS:
12x12 Casserole
Frying Pan
Saucepan

Hudson's Nutmeg
Scalloped Potatoes

6 large Idaho potatoes
1 lb. bacon, chopped
2 large yellow onions, peeled and julienned
1 quart cream
1 1/2 teaspoons black pepper
1 1/2 teaspoons white pepper
1 tablespoon nutmeg
4 tablespoons cornstarch mixed with 3–4 tablespoons water
Salt to taste
1 tablespoon butter
1/2 cup Parmesan, grated

1. Put potatoes in a large saucepan with cold water to cover. Bring to a boil.
2. Boil potatoes in jackets until done but still firm.
3. Cool and remove skin. Cut lengthwise and then across in 1/2" slices.
4. Place in buttered baking dish or casserole, overlapping rows of slices like shingles on a roof.
5. Brown bacon, drain, and reserve drippings.
6. Sauté onions in 2 tablespoons bacon drippings in the same pan. Combine with bacon.
7. Combine cream, peppers, and nutmeg in a clean saucepan over medium heat.
8. Bring to a boil and add cornstarch slurry to make sauce. It's better for it to be too thick than too thin. Stir and adjust seasoning.
9. Sprinkle bacon-onion mixture over potatoes. Top with sauce, nd sprinkle with Parmesan.
10. Bake at 400°, 30–45 minutes until bubbling and browned.

"Potato Head Blues" —Louis Armstrong

You can't go wrong with the born-to-be-together combination of bacon-onion-potato. Add cream and nutmeg and you'll find yourself pickin' at the crust.

Balsamic Asparagus

They're bright, they're green, they're lying at 12 o'clock on your plate. What can I say about asparagus? People who like it really like it, those who don't—well, you know who you are.

Balsamic vinegar is so renowned that it has reached almost cult status. Produced from the Lambrusco grape, *the* vine in Italy, it has a sweet, rich, acidity. All sorts of legends abound of how, when the moon is full, the grapes are squeezed by monks, or was it virgins?

All of a sudden the world is consuming more balsamic vinegar than can be produced. We only discovered it 10 years ago and some is aged 50–60 years to achieve its true glory. Do the math and enjoy it while you can.

The more this vinegar ages the richer it becomes. Besides its obvious uses with vegetables and salads, you can even dip strawberries in it. Some restaurants have even started serving it as a liqueur.

Cooking asparagus is like a trip to a Sandinavian spa—out of the heat and into an icy bath—so refreshing and you feel so crisp.

"Norweigan Wood"
—The Beatles

VARIATIONS: Green beans, yellow squash, zucchini, blanched broccoli, or aspiration (a cross between asparagus and broccoli).

TIMING: Cook asparagus early in the day. Cool and reserve.

TOOLS:
6-Quart Pot
Chef's Knife
Sauté Pan

Balsamic Asparagus

2 bunches asparagus
3 quarts water
1/4 cup sugar
1 1/2 cups good balsamic vinegar
2 tablespoons garlic, minced
2 tablespoons red onion, minced
1/4 cup brown sugar, packed
1 teaspoon fresh basil
1 teaspoon fresh oregano
1/2 teaspoon fresh thyme
1 tablespoon salt
1 teaspoon white pepper
1/2 cup white wine
1/4 lb. butter

1. Trim the ends off the asparagus. Bend an asparagus spear while holding each end. Cut it where it snaps.
2. Boil water and sugar
3. Plunge the cut asparagus into the boiling sugar water for approximately 4 minutes. The sugar helps to strengthen the cell walls of the asparagus and hold the green, so you will have shockingly bright vegetables. Drain quickly.
4. Plunge the hot asparagus into a bowl of ice water. This will stop the cooking and brighten the color even more. Leave the spears in the ice water about the same length of time they were cooked. Drain and reserve.
5. Put all the other ingredients in a sauté pan and simmer for 5 minutes. Add the asparagus.
6. Simmer for 3–4 minutes and serve immediately.

The mysterious dark flavors of balsamic vinegar stand up to the strength of asparagus.

Ancho Bock Beer
Smashers

Serves 6–8, but it's rarely enough

This is a Hudson's signature dish. We serve it with many of our entrées and people never seem to get tired of it. I think it was Michael Fritch who said he always put beer in his potatoes. A skeptical Jay replied, "Oh, sure," in his most sarcastic voice and then went right around the corner and tried it himself. Son of a gun, another dimension in taste!

This must have gone to his head, because soon thereafter Jay got feeling frisky and decided to experiment further. Keep in mind that this was in the heyday of unusual potato combinations—garlic, horseradish, green pea guacamole, whatever. So Jay naturally reached for ancho chilies. When Jeff came up and saw what he was doing, he had only one thing to say—"double the amount" . . . and so a Hudson's classic was born.

Potatoes love to party. If you can add beer to potatoes, what else can you add?

"In heaven there is no beer and so we drink it here" (and cook with it)

VARIATION: Support your local micro-brewery. Anchor Steam on the west coast is good. Genesee Cream Ale is dandy for people in the east. Just avoid anything with "lite" on the label.

TOOLS:
Electric Mixer
Ricer
Blender

TIMING: If you anticipate a time crunch you can peel the potatoes a day ahead, but the whole dish is better when prepared *a la minute*. They taste great the next day if you're lucky enough to have 'em.

Ancho Chili Bock Beer Smashers

5–6 ancho chili peppers, puréed
2 lbs. Idaho potatoes
1/2 lb. sweet potatoes
1/2 lb. sweet butter, cubed
1/2 cup heavy cream
1/2 bottle Shiner Bock beer, or any big, malty beer
2 teaspoons salt

1. Soak ancho chilies in water to cover until soft. Remove stems, ribs and seeds. Purée with 1/2 cup water in a blender to yield 1/2 cup ancho purée.
2. Peel and boil Idaho potatoes and sweet potatoes until tender. Drain.
3. Warm the beer, cream and butter to slightly above room temperature. Cold milk and cold butter cause the starch in the potatoes to seize up, which is the main cause of glutinous mash potatoes.
4. Whip the Idaho and sweet potatoes together with electric mixer. Add cream, chunks of butter one at a time, ancho purée, beer, and salt.
5. Adjust salt flavor and keep warm until served.

These re-heat well with a little more butter added.

Mashed, malty, a little bit sweet, with a kick of ancho.

Napa Cabbage

Serves 6–8

Fresh, sharp, and smoky.

W hy this is called Napa or Nappa cabbage we cannot say. It is not from Napa Valley, it is not from the auto parts store, and it is not an Italian thing to do after lunch. This is a Chinese cabbage with a pale lime green color and many raised veins. Related to Savoy lettuce, it is also called wong bok, sort of like bok choy. It grows elongated, like a head of romaine, and is about the size of a football. We like it because it maintains a nice little crunch when you eat it.

"Cabbage ... a vegetable about as big and wise as a man's head"
—Ambrose Bierce

"Cabbage Head" —*Professor Longhair*

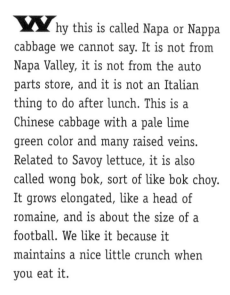

VARIATIONS: Oriental kale, Savoy lettuce, wilted spinach, collard greens, mustard greens. For all you vegetarians, leave out the bacon.

TOOLS:
Large Sauté Pan

TIMING: Chop all your veggies early but heat and mix just before serving.

Napa Cabbage

3 tablespoons butter
2 tablespoons cracked black pepper
4 tablespoons garlic, chopped
1/2 cup cooked bacon, diced
2 tablespoons Bronze Rub
    (see Salt and Seasoning section, p. xx)
2 tablespoons brown sugar
1/4 cup rice wine vinegar
1 red onion, julienned
1 red bell pepper, julienned
1 poblano chili, peeled, seeded, and julienned
1 head Napa cabbage, sliced lengthwise then
    cut across in 1" slices
Salt to taste

1. Combine butter, pepper, garlic, bacon, Bronze Rub, brown sugar, and vinegar in a large sauté pan. Bring to a boil.
2. Add red onion, red bell pepper, and poblano. Sauté until tender. Toss in sliced Napa cabbage until it just wilts.
3. Taste and adjust seasonings. Serve immediately.

Hudson's Variable Veggies

Serves 8

The rich butter and bacon balanced by the wine and vinegar opens all the tastebuds to receive the flavors of the veggies in their garlic, herb seasoning.

Making tempting vegetables for restaurant consumption is a challenge. You don't want children in the dining room whining plaintively, "How many bites do I have to eat before I can have dessert?" This recipe is a tastebud bullseye—salty, sweet, sour and bitter—rounding all the bases before sliding into home.

VARIATIONS: Yes! That's the point. What's in season, what you like. Mix up the herb butter mixture and put it on any vegetable. You can cook virtually any vegetable in this—peppers, onions, tomatoes, green beans, mixed vegetables, squash, broccoli, red bells, julienned carrots.

TIMING: 5 minutes before service, sauté and slather.

TOOLS: Sauté Pan

Hudson's Variable Veggies

3 tablespoons bacon, cooked and chopped
1 tablespoon garlic, chopped
1 tablespoon red onion, chopped
3 tablespoons chablis
1/4 cup rice wine vinegar
1/2 stick butter
3 tablespoons brown sugar
1/2 tablespoon salt
1/2 tablespoon cracked black pepper
1 teaspoon each of dried basil, oregano, thyme
4 cups of mixed squashes

1. Chop your squash medley into 1/4" slices to insure even cooking.
2. Fry bacon, drain, chop and set aside.
3. Simmer all ingredients except squash in sauté pan until well blended (3–4 minutes)
4. Add squash of your choice, cook until just tender.

To eat is human, to digest, divine.
—Mark Twain

"Call Any Vegetable" —Frank Zappa

Bourbon Vanilla Praline
Sweet Potatoes

Serves 12

I't all started out with Jeff's "no marshmallow" rule. Maybe he had a bad marshmallow experience in his youth, who knows, but he feels very strongly about not wanting them in his sweet potatoes. This is a very good rule except for those who know, deep in their hearts, that sweet potatoes can only be cooked with marshmallows. In which case we say, "It's YOUR kitchen."

But anyway, back in Jeff's kitchen, there was sauce a-brewing. It started out as a bubblin' brandy sauce for the cheese cake and then suddenly we were swept away to Madagascar—off the coast of Africa—where the truly great vanilla is grown, most specifically on Bourbon Island. Bourbon vanilla beans are the "ne plus ultra" of vanilla beanage and worth their weight in gold. Legend has it that the Spanish brought these beans from Mexico. Unfortunately they were unable to successfully transplant the vanilla "bee" necessary for pollination.

The orchid that produces this exquisite bean opens for only an hour in its entire life—which means you can't be waiting around for some bee that may or may not show up. So, every flower is hand pollinated—with a crew of pollinators standing by in anticipation of the golden moment. The flowers produce a long green bean that has to be dried in the sun for days and days. Anyway, you get the idea that this is a labor-intensive process and a feeling for why vanilla beans are so expensive.

As we were experimenting with the sauce, we remembered the wonderfulness of pralines—that sweet pecan candy with cinnamon and brown sugar. Whether you first tasted them as a treat in New Orleans, or along the highways of America at Stuckey's, it's a taste worth remembering. So, the Bourbon Vanilla Praline Sauce was born—and we discovered the perfect accompaniment to sweet potatoes.

We brake for pralines.

"Brown Sugar"
—The Rolling
Stones

VARIATIONS: Throw out the sweet potatoes and put this sauce over anything that could benefit from these flavors—waffles, pancakes, pound cake, apple pies, cheese cake, vanilla ice cream, pralines & cream ice cream, a huge spoon, your finger...you get the idea.

TIMING: This dish can be prepared the day before and then heated prior to serving.

TOOLS:
Saucepan
Casserole Dish
Paring Knife

Bourbon Vanilla Praline Sweet Potatoes

6 large sweet potatoes
1 1/2 cups graham cracker crumbs
2 tablespoons butter
1 1/2 cups pecan pieces
2 cups Hudson's Bourbon Vanilla Praline Sauce
OR 2 cups of sauce made from the following recipe

1. Place sweet potatoes in saucepan with cold water to cover. Boil sweet potatoes until just done.
2. Drain and set aside until cool enough to handle. Remove the skins with a paring knife. Chill.
3. Slice lengthwise into two pieces, then slice across into 1/4" slices
4. Arrange in a well-buttered casserole dish.
5. Warm praline sauce, ours or yours, in a water bath or microwave. Drizzle over the top.
6. Sprinkle top with graham cracker crumbs, then pecans.
7. Bake in a 350° oven for 35 minutes or until its hot and bubbling.

Bourbon Vanilla Praline Sauce

1 quart light corn syrup
1/3 cup vanilla extract (preferably Bourbon vanilla)
2 tablespoons and 1 teaspoon rum extract
2 tablespoons cinnamon, ground
1 tablespoon nutmeg, ground
2 lbs. brown sugar
1/3 cup brandy (drinkable but not VSOP)
1/2 lb. butter, whole, unsalted
2 cups pecan pieces

1. Combine all ingredients except pecans in a saucepan.
2. Cook until bubbling, then add 2 cups pecans.

Sweet, nutty, and spicy — all the flavors of the holiday season in one dish.

DESSERTS

The best way to deal with temptation is to give in to it.

Crumbled Apple with Bubbling Brandy Butter

Texas Lemon Bomb—a Tribute to Ann Richards

Hudson's Turtle Pie—Our Best Mistake

Tina Turner Mousse

Sour Cherry Carrot Cake

Chocolate Heat or Cinco "C" Brownies

Quatro Leches Cake with Kahlua Mousse

Chocolate Raspberry Torte with Chocolate Ganache Topping

Passion Fruit Crème Brûlée

Champagne Herb Sorbet

Canela White Chocolate Ice Cream— The World's Richest

Crumbled Apple

with Bubbling Brandy Butter

Serves 6

It was probably Sir Isaac Newton who first had the idea for this dessert, but as always we have been able to improve on the original by the diligent application of a wonderful sauce. When this fabulous dessert comes bubbling through the restaurant, a chain reaction begins and soon the kitchen is overwhelmed with orders for more of "what he's having."

The secret is to serve it on a hot iron skillet so all the flavors waft through the dining room. A scoop of homemade ice cream on the side never hurts.

Freelance food writer Vance Muse tells us that once he worked up his nerve to ask Julia Child about her passionate use of butter. She paused for a moment and replied, "Vance, if you remove butter from your diet, you'll be buried alive in dandruff." We never argue with Julia.

"Bubblin' Up" —Dr. Hook

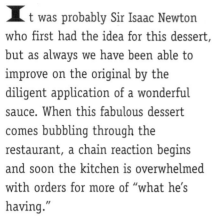

VARIATION: Golden raisins make a nice substitute for the dried cherries.

TIMING: Bubbling Brandy Butter can be made days in advance, and the apples can be prepared the morning before serving.

TOOLS: Apple Corer, Spoon or Melon Baller, Saucepan, Paring Knife, Food Processor, Hot Iron Skillet or Ceramic Casserole for service

Crumbled Apple

6 Granny Smith apples
1 cup dried cherries
3 oz. dark rum
1 cup granulated sugar
1 cup brown sugar, packed
1 1/2 cups flour
1 cup almond slivers
1 1/2 teaspoons cinnamon
1/2 teaspoon nutmeg
1 lb. butter, chilled and cubed
Dash of salt
Bubbling Brandy Butter

1. Preheat oven to 400°.
2. Cut top 1/4 off the apple. Remove the center core. With a spoon or melon baller, create a 1 1/2" pocket.
3. Cut 8 evenly spaced slits into the inside of the cored apple with a paring knife. This will allow the flavors and juices to mingle as the apple bakes.
4. Stuff apples with dried cherries. Add 1/2 oz. dark rum per apple and set apples aside.
5. Mix sugar, brown sugar, flour, almonds, cinnamon, nutmeg, and butter in food processor for crumble mix. Pulse no more than 20 seconds. Butter should be chunky.
6. Top apples with crumble mix packing it into a dome with the palm of your hand. Bake in preheated oven for 15 minutes.
7. Top with Bubbling Brandy Butter.

Bubblin' Brandy Butter (Bubba-Lynn)

1 cup brandy
1/2 cup rum
1/2 lb. butter
1/2 cup vanilla
1/2 tablespoon cinnamon
1 cup cream
2 cups sugar
1/2 teaspoon nutmeg

1. Combine brandy and rum in a medium saucepan and heat. Ignite alcohol, and flame until reduced by half. The brandy and rum should be of good enough quality to consume (we prefer dark rum for the added flavor). Caution, 2 cups of burning alcohol is hot and dangerous. Have a lid nearby to smother it. Do not try to pick-up or carry a flaming pot of alcohol.
2. Add all the other ingredients in any order. Return to a rolling boil for three minutes. Then set aside until the apples are baked.
3. Heat a small cast iron skillet over high heat or in the oven. We use the ones with no handle. When very hot, center the apple on the pan, pour the sauce over and watch it bubble.

One can taste this dish before it gets to the table—baked apples, cinnamon, vanilla, rum, and brandy all vaporizing into the air.

Texas Lemon Bomb

A Tribute to Ann Richards with that "Cotton Candy" Hair

Serves 8 generously

Former Governor Ann Richards is a Texas icon. And her hair, well, big hair is a Texas tradition and since Ann's looks like a dessert, we decided to make a dessert that looks like Ann.

Actually we started out to make Baked Alaska but it kind of got away from us. We had this bombe mold and as we layered it, it began to look more and more like a head—and then hair became the next logical addition—and then the head started to look familiar. It's such a great dessert, we think you'll vote for it, too.

Great Women Inspire Great Desserts

"Northeast Texas Women" (with that cotton candy hair) —Willis Allen Ramsey

VARIATION: Try lime or orange.

TIMING: This needs to be prepared over two days to allow for freezing.

TOOLS:
4–5 Quart Stainless Steel Bowl or Bombe Mold
Saucepan
Blender
Double Boiler
Whisk
Blow Torch
Pastry Bag
Mixing Bowl

Lemon Custard

1 lb. butter
3 cups granulated sugar
24 egg yolks plus 8 whites
Juice and zest of 12 lemons
3 tablespoons vanilla extract
1/2 gallon rich vanilla ice cream (Ben & Jerry's)

Meringue

16 egg whites
3/4 cup powdered sugar
3 tablespoons 151-proof rum or Everclear (optional)

1. Melt 1 lb. butter in a saucepan. Whisk in 3 cups sugar, and heat until dissolved and very hot.
2. Combine 24 egg yolks and 8 egg whites with lemon juice, lemon zest, and vanilla extract in a blender. Blend at high speed. Begin to add hot butter and sugar mixture—slowly at first, then faster until all has been added.
3. Transfer the blender mixture, while still hot, to a double boiler and whisk over simmering water until ribbons of sauce lay on top–like Hollandaise. Set aside to cool in an ice bath or refrigerate.
4. In the bottom of a bombe mold or large stainless, glass, or plastic bowl, smash softened ice cream about 2 inches thick.
5. Smooth out the ice cream layer with a spatula or your hands. Add 2 inches of cooled lemon custard and quickly place in freezer.
6. Approximately 3 hours later repeat this layer process. You will have 2 ice cream and 2 lemon custard layers. Return to the freezer overnight.

The next day:
7. Whip 16 egg whites and 3/4 cup powdered sugar until stiff but not dry. Remove bombe from freezer and remove from bombe mold or bowl. Using a pastry bag filled with meringue, give your dessert an Ann Richards hairdo.
8. Return to freezer for 3 hours minimum, or until just before serving.
9. Remove from freezer. Brown the meringue with a blowtorch or warm 3 tablespoons of 151 rum in the microwave, pour on top and light. Be careful! This is dangerous, but a real Texas show stopper!

Sharp, cool, and sweet.

Hudson's
Turtle Pie

Our Best Mistake
Makes 1 pie—8 servings

One night Jay was making pecan pies—ten of them to be exact. He was simmering the filling on the stove, and then the phone rang. Well, it must have been something important because the phone call went on a long time. Meanwhile the filling continued to boil, and boil, and boil some more. When he looked back at the mixture, it had gone into what candy makers call its "softball stage," great for candy, bad news for pie filling.

But Jay is not the kind of guy to throw away ten pies. So he went ahead and put the "softball" filling into the pie shells and baked them. Sure enough, after they cooled, he tried to slice one and all the filling ran out.

Still unwilling to throw away all those pies, Jay put the mixture into the freezer. There were those who thought he might be trying to hide the evidence.

The next day, he sliced the pies and dipped each piece in Belgian chocolate, encasing the soft filling. Mmmmm . . . and the rest, as they say, is history. The Hudson's Turtle Pie was born.

"A chef is like a general, it takes a mishap to reveal his genius."
–Horace.

"My Favorite Mistake"
—Sheryl Crow

VARIATION:
Dip strawberries, cherries or other fruits in the dipping chocolate

TIMING:
Can be done days in advance and shipped out across the country.

TOOLS:
Saucepan, Wax Paper or Parchment, Mixing Bowls, Double Boiler or Mixing Bowl on Top of Saucepan, Dipping Fork, Plastic Film

Hudson's Turtle Pie

1 cup light corn syrup
1/2 stick of butter
1 cup light brown sugar, packed
1 cup granulated sugar
5 egg yolks
2 tablespoons vanilla extract
2 tablespoons flour
1 1/4 cups pecan pieces
2 tablespoons plus 2 teaspoons corn oil or hazelnut oil
large deep pie shell

1. Preheat oven to 300°.
2. Combine corn syrup, butter, granulated sugar, and brown sugar in a saucepan over medium to high heat. Bring mixture to a boil.
3. Reduce heat and let mixture simmer, stirring occasionally for 15 minutes or until sugars are dissolved and color begins to deepen.
4. Combine egg yolks and vanilla in a mixing bowl, beating lightly with a fork to blend.
5. Remove pan containing hot syrup from heat.
6. Stir a little hot syrup into egg yolks. Immediately pour the egg yolk mixture back into the pot containing the syrup.
7. Stir to blend well. Whip in flour and set aside.
8. Fill pie shell with pecan pieces. Pour syrup into pie shell.
9. Place pie in center of a cookie sheet in case of overflow. Bake at 300° for 20–25 minutes or until edges are bubbling but center is still a little loose.
10. Cool pie. Place in airtight container and freeze overnight.
11. Slice pie into eight even slices while frozen. Jab it with a fork and dip it into the Dipping Chocolate, scraping the excess chocolate off the bottom of the crust. Drop the encrusted pie onto wax or parchment paper and refrigerate. You can get a rhythm going here—stab, dunk, scrape, and drop.

Dipping Chocolate

1 lb. dark semi-sweet chocolate
3 1/2 tablespoons light canola oil

1. Heat chocolate over simmering water in a bowl covered tightly with plastic film until warm. Whisk oil into the chocolate.
2. Keeping chocolate warm, dip pie slices into the chocolate mix.
3. Place dipped pie slices on wax or parchment paper and refrigerate.

Slice through the chocolate and get a slow ooze of pecan, brown sugar wonderfulness.

Tina Turner Mousse

Serves 6

Making a dessert in honor of an entertainer is as old as Escoffier. He created Peach Melba in 1899 as a tribute to Madame Nellie Melba, the great diva, commemorating the swan from the first act of *Lohengrin*. An Australian dessert is named for the Russian ballerina, Anna Pavlova, a confection of meringue, whipped cream, passion fruit, kiwi and pineapple.

This dessert is dedicated to a contemporary diva, Tina Turner, a performer known for her unforgettable voice and great legs. "Legs" is also the term used to describe streams of wine that cling and then slide down the inside of a glass when wine is swirled. In this dish it is swirling chocolate making a tempting presentation, a fitting tribute, and a great tasting dessert.

The best way to deal with temptation is to give into it.

"She's Got Legs" —ZZ Top

VARIATION: If you don't have Chambord, try Grand Marnier, Frambroise, or Tuaca.

TIMING: Best if made no earlier than the morning of your dinner party.

TOOLS: Saucepan, Double Boiler, Whisk, Electric Mixer, Wine Glasses, Mixing Bowl, Pastry Bag

Chambord Mousse

1 cup Chambord liqueur
4 oz. semi-sweet chocolate
2 cups heavy cream
1/2 cup granulated sugar
1 pint raspberries

1. In a small saucepan, simmer liqueur until reduced to 1/4 cup, and cool.
2. Melt chocolate in a double boiler or in a bowl over simmering water. Stir until smooth and transfer into stainless bowl. Hold at room temperature.
3. Whip the heavy cream and sugar in a well-chilled bowl with an electric mixer. As the cream begins to form soft peaks, add the Chambord syrup in a slow steady stream. Stop mixing at medium-firm peaks.
4. Take 1 cup of the Chambord whipped cream and fold it into the chocolate. Vigorously whisk the two together until well blended. This will keep the chocolate from seizing up when blending with cold whipped cream mixture.
5. Add the chocolate cream mixture to the remaining whipped cream and gently fold together until smooth.
6. Chill for two hours.

Chocolate Fudge

2 cups cream
1/2 stick butter
1 cup brown sugar
1 cup granulated sugar
1/4 teaspoon salt
2 cups Dutch cocoa, sifted

1. In a saucepan, combine heavy cream and butter. Bring to a boil.
2. Add brown and granulated sugars and salt.
3. Bring back to a boil and stir, making sure all the sugar is dissolved.
4. Remove from the heat and whisk in cocoa, 1/2 cup at a time.
5. Whisk vigorously until all cocoa has been added. Hold at warm room temperature, or near warm stove.
6. Make "legs of fudge" in a wine glass or tall parfait.
7. Load a pastry bag with chilled mousse and fill fudged wine glass 1/2 full.
8. Garnish with raspberries.

Ah, the thrill of eating your way through a light chocolate cloud only to find a dark, rich puddle of chocolate at the bottom.

Sour Cherry Carrot Cake

1 20-lb. cake, or 20 1-lb. servings—serves at least 12 people

Beware! This Cake is Addictive.
Some say it ought to be declared illegal. In fact . . . there was this one time when Jeff was supposedly on a diet, and the alarm system at the restaurant went off in the middle of the night. Hudson's is just down the road from where he lives, so Jeff went to investigate.

All the doors were locked and no one appeared to be around, but he went inside to check further. While he was there, he just *happened* to check inside the cooler—a logical place for an intruder to hide? And just *happened* to pick up a piece of this cake.

Locking the door behind him, Jeff headed for his car. Suddenly he was caught in the glare of a large spotlight with a disembodied voice ordering him to put up his hands. Needless to say he obeyed—until they told him to "drop it." Unwilling to give up a piece of sour cherry carrot cake, he plaintively called to the police—"but it's just cake."

Well, he didn't get arrested that time, though he is still a little afraid that the dessert police will catch up with him eventually. While he will usually eat enough of the desserts at the restaurant to tire of them—this one still gets him.

"Never eat more than you can lift."
—Miss Piggy

"So Nice I Tried It Twice" —The O'Jays

VARIATION: Peaches will gladly substitute for mangoes.

TIMING: Cake can be done a day ahead and iced at the last minute. As with all butter cream icings, it is best to serve at room temperature to release all the flavors.

TOOLS:
2 10" Round Cake Pans
Mandoline
Large Sauce Pot
Electric Mixer
Food Processor

3 Large Mixing Bowls
Cake Tester or Toothpick
Whisk
Jogging Shoes

Sour Cherry Carrot Cake

2 cups all purpose flour
2 teaspoons baking soda
2 teaspoons cinnamon
1 tablespoon fresh ginger, minced
1 teaspoon fresh nutmeg, grated
1/2 teaspoon salt
3 whole fresh eggs
3/4 cup mayonnaise
1 1/2 cups granulated sugar
1 cup mango, diced (if fresh is unavailable canned will do)
1/4 cup mango juice (if fresh is unavailable canned will do)
1 cup carrots, peeled and julienned
1 cup jicama, peeled and julienned (if jicama is unavailable substitute more carrots)
1 cup dried sour cherries
1 cup pecan pieces

1. Pre-heat oven to 350°.
2. Grease and flour 2 10" round cake pans.
3. Combine flour, baking soda, cinnamon, ginger, nutmeg, and salt in a mixing bowl. Blend well and set aside.
4. Combine eggs, mayonnaise, sugar, mangoes, and mango juice in another bowl. Blend together with whisk and combine with bowl of dry ingredients.
5. Fold in carrots, jicama, cherries, and pecans.
6. Divide evenly into the two greased and floured cake pans. Bake for 50–55 minutes or until cake tester or toothpick comes out clean.
7. Set aside to cool while making the Sour Cherry and Cream Cheese icing.

An explosion of flavors and textures — tart cherry, and perfume of mangoes, combined with island spice, encased in a sweet creamy richness.

Sour Cherry and Cream Cheese Icing

Before the days of refrigeration, butter and cream icings were designed to seal in the freshness of the cake. It is also possible that the addition of icing made people eat more cake and then you really didn't have to worry about it getting stale.

1/2 lb. butter
1/2 lb. cream cheese
1/2 cup heavy cream
1/2 cup dried sour cherries
1 tablespoon vanilla extract
1 tablespoon Jamaican dark rum
1 lb. powdered sugar

1. Set butter and cream cheese in a mixing bowl at room temperature to soften.
2. Combine heavy cream and cherries in a large sauce pot over medium heat. Heat until cherries are soft and plump, about 7 minutes. Heavy cream likes to boil over as soon as you turn your back—no matter how big the pot. So pay attention.
3. Let cool and transfer to a food processor. Purée with rum and vanilla. Place in refrigerator to cool completely.
4. Cream the butter and cream cheese together with a mixer at medium-high, then add cooled cherry purée.
5. Gradually add the powdered sugar until a pleasing consistency is reached. Then, ice the cake and lick the bowl.
6. Next, go run 5 miles so you can justify eating this cake!!!!!

Chocolate Heat

or Cinco "C" Brownies
10–12 Big Brownies

We didn't think you could improve on chocolate—but we decided to try anyway. While dark mysterious chocolate is rarely seen in the company of a spicy pepper, when they meet you can feel the heat—ooh, la, la.

"Oh, chocolate, my dark master"
–Kramer, on Seinfeld

"I feel the earth move under my feet,"
—Carole King

VARIATIONS: Cascabel peppers are hard to find so go ahead and use ancho peppers.

TIMING: Brownies can be microwaved to reheat.

Chocolate Heat Brownies

6 cascabel peppers
10 oz. semi-sweet chocolate
8 tablespoons unsalted butter
1/2 cup all-purpose flour
4 tablespoons unsweetened cocoa
1/2 teaspoon cayenne pepper
2 teaspoons baking powder
1 teaspoon salt
6 eggs
2 cups sugar
2 teaspoons vanilla
1/2 cup sour cream
2 cups unsalted cashews
1 cup dried cherries.

TOOLS:
9x9x2 Square Cake Pan
Double Boiler
Sifter
Mixing Bowl
Electric Mixer
Plastic Wrap
Blender

1. Preheat oven to 325°.
2. Lightly coat cake pan with butter and dust with flour. Shake out extra flour.
3. Submerge peppers in hot water in a bowl to rehydrate. Cover bowl with plastic wrap and let stand for approximately 15 minutes. Drain and remove seeds.
4. In a double boiler, melt chocolate and butter over water at a low simmer.
5. Sift flour, cocoa, cayenne pepper, baking powder, and salt together and set aside.
6. Put seeded cascabel peppers in a blender and purée until smooth.
7. Place eggs, sugar and vanilla in a mixing bowl. Mix at high speed until slightly thick, approximately 2 minutes.
8. Add chocolate-butter mixture and pepper blend to mixer bowl along with eggs and sugar. Beat on medium high for 1 1/2 minutes.
9. Next, add sifted ingredients and mix for one minute on medium speed.
10. Add sour cream and mix on medium speed for 30 seconds. Fold in cashews and dried cherries.
11. Pour into cake pan.
12. Place in pre-heated oven and bake for 45–55 minutes.
13. Remove and cool for 20 minutes.

Best if served warm with Homemade Cinnamon Ice Cream and Fudge Sauce from Tina Turner Mousse.

First is the chocolate and then later a tiny firecracker goes off in your mouth.

Quatro Leches
Cake

with Kahlua Mousse
Serves 10

This is a traditional Mexican dessert which is sometimes called drunken cake. Originally it was "Tres" Leches cake but we added goat's milk to up the ante. The Kahlua Mousse can stand alone as a dessert, but what could be better than two desserts—one on top of the other.

VARIATION:
Delete goat's milk and add rice milk or buttermilk.

TIMING:
Make the Kahlua Mousse the day before and chill.

TOOLS:
Saucepan, Whisk, Cake Pan 9x9x2, Cake Tester or Toothpick, Electric Mixer, Sifter, Mixing Bowls, Double Boiler, Pastry Bag, Star Tip

Cake

1 cup flour
1/3 cup cocoa
1 teaspoon baking powder
1/2 teaspoon salt
1 cup sugar
5 eggs
1/4 cup water
1 tablespoon vanilla

1. Preheat oven to 400°.
2. Sift flour, cocoa, baking powder and salt together and set aside.
3. In a mixer, blend sugar and eggs about 3 minutes until light and frothy.
4. Add vanilla and water. Blend on high until fluffy and about twice the original size in volume, approximately 10 minutes on high.
5. Next quickly fold in dry ingredients and pour into buttered cake pan.
6. Bake 12–15 minutes.
7. Fork or tester should come out clean.
8. Remove and cool.

Quatro Leches

2 tablespoons cocoa
1 tablespoon instant coffee
1/4 cup sugar
1/2 cup Kahlua
1/2 cup goat's milk
1 cup heavy cream
1 can condensed milk (14 oz.)
1 can evaporated milk (12 oz.)

1. Whisk cocoa, instant coffee, sugar and Kahlua together in a saucepan and simmer for 3 minutes. Set aside to cool.
2. Blend the four milks in a mixing bowl. Add cooled coffee mixture and whisk together.
3. Slide a knife around the cake pan and poke several dozen holes in the cake with a cake tester or toothpick. Pour milk mixture slowly over the cake until it can't absorb any more. You may have a little milk mixture left over.*
4. Cut into squares and top with Kahlua Mousse. A dollop is dandy, but if you want to get fancy, put the mousse into a pastry bag and you can make a rosette or any other design you want.

*Add a couple of scoops of ice cream and blend to make the world's best milk shake. (Three desserts in one— we're goin' for the record.)

You can have your cake and drink it too.

"Sweet Dreams are Made of This . . ."
— Eurythmics

Kahlua Mousse

1 cup Kahlua
2 tablespoons instant coffee
4 oz. semi-sweet chocolate
2 cups heavy cream
1/2 cup granulated sugar

1. Combine Kahlua and instant coffee in a saucepan and reduce until 1/2 cup remains. Cool and reserve.
2. Melt chocolate over a simmering water bath or in a double boiler covered with plastic wrap. Stir until smooth and transfer into metal bowl. Cool at room temperature.
3. Whip the heavy cream and sugar in a well-chilled bowl with an electric mixer, slowly adding the cooled Kahlua-coffee mixture into the cream. It will begin to form soft peaks. Stop mixing at medium-firm peaks.
4. Take 1 cup of the whipped cream/sugar/Kahlua mixture and, using a whisk, vigorously whip it into the bowl with the chocolate until the two are well blended. This will keep the chocolate from seizing up when blending with cold whipped cream.
5. Gently fold in the rest of the whipped cream until smooth.
6. Chill for two hours.
7. Fill pastry bag fitted with a star tip and pipe rosettes onto cake pieces.

Chocolate Raspberry Torte

with Chocolate Ganache Topping

8 generous slices

In the early days at Hudson's, most of our desserts came from Texas Tortes, a company run by Dr. Art—a doctor of biochemistry who supplemented his academic income by cooking desserts. Later he went on to author two dessert cookbooks. He graciously gave us this recipe to use as our own.

As a man of science he knew that there are certain flavor partners that were meant to be together. After years of cooking and eating experience, we know that it is a crime to keep chocolate and raspberries apart.

Brillat-Savarin, one of our culinary forefathers, quoted this lecture from a chemistry professor to his cook in *The Physiology of Taste* in 1825: "You are a little opinionated, and I have had some trouble in making you understand that the phenomena which take place in your kitchen are nothing other than the execution of the eternal laws of nature, and that certain things which you do without thinking, and only because you have seen others do them, derive nonetheless from the highest scientific principles."

Opinionated?! *Let's discuss it over dessert.*

Art meets science in the kitchen and it's delicious.

"Love Potion Number 9" —The Searchers

VARIATIONS: Orange and orange zest with reduced Grand Marnier or Frangelico and Almond Butter.

TIMING: This is a no flour cake so it's impossible for it to get stale. Make it several days ahead of time if you want. Just keep it wrapped and refrigerated and out of reach. Camouflage may be necessary.

TOOLS:

Double Boiler *aka*
  Metal Bowl on top
  of simmering
  water
Electric Mixer
Blender
9" Cake Pan

Chocolate Raspberry Torte

10 1/3 oz. chocolate (we use a dark, bittersweet, Belgian type)
10 1/3 oz. butter
5 eggs
2/3 cup sugar
2/3 cup cream
1 pint raspberries (approximately)

1. Melt chocolate in a double boiler over simmering water.
2. When melted, stir in butter until smooth.
3. Remove from heat, cool slightly.
4. Purée raspberries in a blender and strain, until you have 2/3 cup of purée.
5. Combine eggs, sugar, cream, and raspberry purée in mixer and beat until doubled in volume.
6. Add chocolate and blend well.
7. Pour into a 9" cake pan.
8. Bake at 350° for 1 hour and 20 minutes in a water bath.
9. Cool completely before topping with ganache.

Ganache

5 1/2 oz. (or 1 cup) chocolate, shaved
1/2 cup cream

1. Bring cream to a boil in a small saucepan.
2. Add shaved chocolate and stir until smooth.
3. Cool slightly until thickened and pour over torte.
4. Smooth top and sides.

Dark chocolate and tart raspberries, need we say more?

Passion Fruit Crème Brûlée

Serves 6

Rarely satisfied with plain and simple at Hudson's, we decided to augment an already heavenly dessert, Crème Brûlée, with this exotic variation. Truth is, we had this quart of passion fruit juice and were trying to figure out what to do with it. We just figured that anything that tart had to be partnered with something wonderfully sweet.

A passion fruit is a purple egg-shaped fruit about the size of a kiwi. It has edible black seeds and tart orangy pulp. It is ripe just as it begins to wrinkle and needs to be used immediately or it will dry out.

While you may not find this in your produce section, the purée is frequently available in a plastic tub in the frozen fruit juice section.

"You can't get too much crème brûlée" –Jack Lairsen

"Passionate Kisses" —Lucinda Williams

VARIATIONS: Raspberry purée, or orange juice concentrate with a squeeze of lemon or a little ginger and vanilla.

TIMING: You can make the custard the day before and refrigerate. Torch just before service.

TOOLS:
Large Baking Pan
Propane Torch
Strainer
6 Custard Cups
Sauce Pot
Whisk
Mixing Bowl

Passion Fruit Crème Brûlée

18 egg yolks
1/2 cup + 2 tablespoons sugar
2 1/2 cups heavy cream
1/2 cup passion fruit juice (approximately 4–5 passion fruits)
1 vanilla bean, split lengthwise
pinch salt
9 tablespoons sugar for caramelizing (1 1/2 tablespoons per brûlée)

1. Preheat oven to 325°
2. Place egg yolks in a large mixing bowl. Blend lightly.
3. Combine sugar, cream, passion fruit juice, vanilla bean, and a pinch of salt in a large sauce pot over medium-high heat. Bring to a boil.
4. Slowly whisk hot mixture into the egg yolks. This will gradually warm the yolks so you won't have scrambled eggs.
5. Add the warmed yolks back into cream mixture and cook until custard coats the back of a spoon.
6. Strain the mixture.
7. Put the custard cups in a large baking pan and fill the pan with enough *hot* water to come up 1 inch.
8. Fill each custard cup with strained custard. Put the baking pan in the oven and bake at 350° for 35–45 minutes until custard is set. Cool completely.
9. Top each crème brûlée with 1 1/2 tablespoons of sugar and melt/caramelize sugar with a propane torch.
10. Serve with berries or passion fruit sauce, caramelized with a bit of sugar.

Sweet richness offset by the extreme tartness of passion fruit.

Champagne Herb Sorbet

Serves 10

Elegant green ice cream? Champagne sundae? Is it a dessert, a topping for chilled soup, or an intermezzo to clean the palate? All these things and more.

This dish has had a long history at Hudson's. We first invented it as a palate-scrubbing course between the salad and the entrée. It really removes that pesky oil and vinegar from your tastebuds, leaving them ready to receive the main dish. At the end of the meal it's a glamorous lighter-than-air dessert which is also guaranteed to wipe the garlic and onion from your breath.

The secret to this dish is the fresh herbs. You don't have to have an herb garden, just a fresh market supply. We suggest mints, basils, and begonias to make up the majority of the blend, then add a little lemon thyme, lemon balm, sorrel, dill, and tarragon or chervil.

This dish always adds a sense of glamour and excitement to a meal when served in a fancy champagne glass topped with bubbly.

"It's like a mouthful of stars"
—Dom Perignon

VARIATION: Serve on top of chilled fruit soup, floating on a nasturtium leaf or rose petal.

TIMING: Make sorbet the day before and freeze overnight. Check it the next day—if it's too hard to scoop, leave it standing at room temperature for 20 minutes before serving.

TOOLS:
Ice Cream Maker
Zester
Saucepan

Champagne Herb Sorbet

1 1/2 cups granulated sugar
1 1/2 cups water
2 egg whites
2 cups lime juice
zest from 3 limes
1/2 cup champagne for sorbet
3/4 cup herbs, minced (1/2 cup basil and mint, 1/4 cup lemon thyme, lemon balm, sorrel, dill, and tarragon or chervil)
1 bottle of good quality champagne for topping

1. Combine sugar and water in saucepan. Bring to a simmer over medium-high heat until sugar dissolves completely. Cool completely.
2. Add egg whites, lime juice, zest, champagne and minced herbs.
3. Pour into ice cream freezer and freeze according to your machine's directions. Remove from machine and hold in freezer for at least 4 hours.
4. Scoop out sorbet and top with chilled champagne.

"Tiny Bubbles"
—Don Ho

Tartness
of limes and
the bright flavor
of the herbs combine with
the tiny bubbles to add
elegance to any occasion.

Canela White Chocolate Ice Cream

The World's Richest

1 gallon

The proclamation "World's Richest" was awarded by our cooking school participants. Tasting this ice cream caused them to drop their spoons in amazement. The wonderfulness begins with the careful choice of ingredients.

Canela is the best cinnamon with the richest, thinnest bark. White chocolate is cocoa butter with the dark cocoa removed. When looking for a high quality white chocolate, make sure that cocoa butter is the first thing on the ingredient list.

The inspiration for this ice cream came from Blas Gonzales, one of our sous chefs. Blas is from San Luis Potosi, two hours north of Mexico City. His mother used to make a cinnamon milk drink for him and his brothers. It sounded so good, we decided to change the milk to heavy cream (hey, it's what we do) and try it as a frozen treat.

You can't be too rich.

"Baby, You Rich"
—The Mighty Blues Kings

VARIATION: Put this on top of the following: Turtle Pie, Chocolate Heat Brownies, or Crumbled Apple with Bubbling Brandy Butter.

TIMING: This recipe is best made a day in advance, so it has time to harden in the freezer.

TOOLS:
Mixing Bowls
Ice Cream Maker
Saucepan
Whisk
Strainer or Wire Sieve
Large Heavy-bottomed Pot

Canela White Chocolate Ice Cream

Makes approximately 1 gallon—how many servings is that to you?

1 quart cream
8 cinnamon sticks
3 cups white chocolate shavings
1/2 gallon Cream Anglaise

1. Combine cream and cinnamon sticks in a small saucepan.
2. Bring to a boil, remove from heat, and let steep for 30 minutes.
3. Return to a boil and strain into a mixing bowl containing white chocolate shavings. Allow to sit for 2–3 minutes. Then stir to a smooth consistency.
4. Combine with Cream Anglaise *(see recipe below)*.
5. Using your ice cream freezer of choice (and they're all different), freeze according to manufacturer's directions.

Cream Anglaise

15 egg yolks
16 oz. heavy cream
1 quart milk
2 vanilla beans, split
4 cups sugar

1. Place egg yolks into a mixing bowl and set aside.
2. Combine cream, milk, vanilla beans, and sugar in a large heavy-bottomed pot.
3. Bring to a boil.
4. Slowly add hot mixture to egg yolks while whisking vigorously until you have added approximately 2/3 of the mixture to the yolks.
5. Return the egg yolk and cream mixture to the remaining mix in the original pot and cook until you see the first bubble break the surface.
6. Remove, strain through wire sieve and cool.

Con Te Partirò

STOCK OPTIONS

Most of our soups and some of our sauces call for stocks. Technically a stock is a flavored liquid. If you use chicken bones to flavor that liquid, usually water, then you have chicken stock. If you use a rock, then you have a stone stock—the base for stone soup.

Of course, you could substitute water for stock in these recipes, but in the end it would result in heartache. The use of stocks in cooking adds depth and intricacy to the taste. It is one of the layers of flavor. Try your next batch of rice with all chicken stock or vegetable stock instead of water. You'll be thrilled at the depth of flavor that is bestowed on the simple rice grain.

When we walk into the restaurant on Monday or Tuesday when Blas Gonzales is making stock, we're immediately taken with the warm rich smells waltzing through the kitchen. It triggers the olfactory senses that fire up on Thanksgiving when the turkey stock is simmering away for giblet gravy.

Stocks may seem intimidating because you think you need to make the stock fresh before you start the recipe . . . not so! On a quarterly or semi-annual basis take time to make, reduce, and freeze your stocks. This way you'll always be ready to make some great food. You don't go to the mill when you need a cup of flour, you have it in your pantry! Think of stock the same way.

If freezer space is limited, simmer more of the liquid/water out of the strained stock. You can easily make 1 gallon of stock into a 1/2 gallon and save the space. But we warn you, your stock will be sooo rich and intense you will never want to go back to the diluted kind. Guess what—you will be on your way to being a better cook.

If you are new to making stock, fear not. Just follow the steps and you'll do fine. Be sure to taste your stocks and refine your technique the next time around. If your brown veal stock isn't rich and brown, roast the bones longer next time. Cooks practice their craft, so keep practicing.

One more note, *never salt your stocks*. They're used as a flavor ingredient and you may be required to reduce them (which in turn would make them saltier). Adjust your seasoning at the end of the process; that way you are fearlessly in control.

Brown Veal Stock

Yield 1 gallon

1/2 cup vegetable oil
8 lbs. veal bones, browned (we use lots of wild game bones, as well)
1 lb. mirepoix, browned—50% onion, chopped; 25% celery, chopped; 25% carrots, chopped
2–3 oz. tomato paste
4 cloves garlic, whole
1 tablespoon whole black peppercorns
3 bay leaves
2 cups burgundy
6 quarts water

1. Preheat oven to 400°.
2. Place bones in a single layer in a large pre-heated pan with 1/2 cup of oil. Roast 2 hours.
3. Add mirepoix and tomato paste in the last twenty minutes to caramelize.
4. Transfer all to stock pot and deglaze pan with burgundy.
5. Scrape fond (the brown bits stuck to the bottom) from roasting pan and add to stock pot.
6. Cover everything in stock pot with cold water and bring to a boil.
7. Reduce to a simmer.
8. Skim scum periodically.
9. Simmer six hours, adding more water to cover bones as needed.
10. Strain and refrigerate or cool.

If you want deeper, richer stock, keep simmering, but do not reduce over 50% more

Poultry Stock

Yield 1 gallon

8 lbs. chicken or any game bird, bones and carcass
6 quarts water
1 lb. mirepoix—50% onion, chopped; 25% carrot, chopped; 25% celery, chopped
12 black peppercorns
3 bay leaves
1 bunch parsley stems

1. Combine all ingredients in stock pot.
2. Bring to a boil, skim the scum.
3. Reduce to a simmer and cook for 3 hours.
4. Strain and refrigerate or freeze.

Hudson's on the Bend
GOURMET SAUCES

Our special line of sauces are gourmet sauces of restaurant quality. In fact they appear on our world-renowned menu nightly. The sauces were designed to be added at the end of the cooking process, whether it be grilled, roasted, broiled or smoked. We call them finishing sauces because, in most cases, they are not cooked or marinated with the food, but are added just before serving to compliment or finish the entrée. Here are a few serving ideas.

APPLE CIDER BRANDY

Warm and serve with any pork dish. Peel and dice fresh apple in the sauce just before topping a grilled pork chop or pork tenderloin . . . they'll think you've been cooking for hours. (Hide the bottle.) This one is also tasty with chicken, lamb or turkey. It's great with roasted game birds, such as duck, dove, or quail.

BOURBON VANILLA PRALINE

This is our only dessert sauce. We serve it warm over cheesecake. It is also irresistible over ice cream, apple pie, waffles, brownies, or even holiday sweet potatoes.

CHAMPAGNE HERB VINEGAR

This vinegar is a blend of my favorite herbs and spices—sweet basil, lemon thyme, garlic, pink peppercorns, and a fresh hot pepper. It makes any salad dressing better and any recipe calling for vinegar more flavorful.

CHIPOTLE BBQ SAUCE

In this non-traditional barbeque sauce there are lots of garlic and onions with the chipotles to bring a hot, spicy barbeque to life. Enjoy this on all kinds of grilled or smoked meats, or seafoods.

GUAVA SOUR CHERRY

We serve this with grilled venison and other game dishes. It is also excellent with duck or ham. As with our other sauces, warm and serve atop any finished meat.

MADAGASCAR PEPPERCORN SAUCE

This is our red meat steak sauce. It has lots of garlic, shallots, and burgundy, along with the peppery green Madagascar peppercorn. Serve with any steak and instantly turn it into Steak au Poivre. This hearty sauce is fabulous with game. Just warm and serve with your entrée.

MANGO JALAPEÑO

Warm and serve with a grilled pork chop or tenderloin. It is excellent with lamb or chicken. After cooking your entrée, just warm and serve the mango jalapeño. We also serve it with egg rolls, or sauté shrimp in the sauce. Try topping cream cheese and crackers with this chilled sauce. Garnish with fresh mangoes for that extra touch.

MEXICAN MARIGOLD MINT HONEY MUSTARD

This makes any sandwich a special treat. . . or mix with honey and vinegar for a honey mustard salad dressing. Serve warmed over spinach with bacon bits and chopped hard boiled egg for a tasty salad.

ORANGE GINGER BBQ SAUCE

Like the other barbeque, this is a non-traditional sauce that is both versatile and extremely flavorful. Use creatively on all meats and game birds.

STRAWBERRY/RASPBERRY SAUCE

We serve atop grilled pheasant with fresh berries sprinkled on top. There are lots of garlic, shallots, and chardonnay to give this sauce its special zing. This does wonders to baked, broiled, or grilled chicken, or to any game bird. Just warm and serve atop your favorite poultry—it's great with pork loins too.

TOMATILLO WHITE CHOCOLATE

We serve it warm over grilled, broiled, or baked fish and shrimp. It does wonders to grilled chicken, or use it to top off your favorite enchiladas or omelette. I like it chilled with tortilla chips. This is truly a versatile sauce . . . just use your imagination. Remember, it contains only a small amount of Belgium white chocolate. This is not a sweet sauce. Some call it a mole.

HUDSON'S MIXED GIFT PACK

Tomatillo White Chocolate, Mango Jalapeño, Mexican Marigold Mint Mustard, and Bourbon Vanilla Praline . . . all wrapped in an attractive wooden crate. An excellent idea for the gourmets in your life.

BBQ GIFT CRATE

Chipotle and Orange Ginger BBQ sauces packed in a wooden crate, perfect for gift giving.

HUDSON'S ON THE BEND
GOURMET SAUCES
1-800-996-7655

Hudson's on the Bend
COOKING SCHOOL

Hudson's cooking school was born about six years ago and was held at the restaurant on a Sunday morning.

Our first menu was Smoked Quail Salad, Pheasant Tortilla Soup, Venison Stuffed with Smoked Lobster, Corn Pudding, Hudson's Potatoes, and Cheesecake with Praline Sauce.

One of the goals of that first class was to demystify some of the techniques of cooking wild game. Since one of our favorite methods

is smoking—we led the class on a short field trip to the smokehouse. On the way to the smokehouse we went by way of the garden. Someone asked, "What is that over there?" and after a few more questions we found ourselves in the middle of an impromptu tutorial on organic gardening. Each of our classes took us down new paths and helped us expand our own learning. The cooking school classes went so well and we had so much fun that they became regular events, frequently sold out months in advance.

There were benefits we could not have imagined when we started. One was that we were pushed to begin experimenting with new dishes. The classes gave us an opportunity to collaborate and be creative in a way that we might not have had under the day-to-day pressures of running a restaurant. These new recipes appeared on the restaurant menu and were enthusiastically received, which sparked our creativity even more. Secondly, the classes fulfilled our passion for cooking. To cook what we wanted for twenty-five people, using the best ingredients and having the opportunity to show off while doing so, was pretty darn close to chef nirvana.

The cooking school classes took on a life of their own. A nucleus of regular students come back time and again. Some are hunters who want to do something delicious and adventurous with their catch. Others are already good cooks who want to expand their skills. And some come just to enjoy the camaraderie and good food. In some ways it has become more of a social event; we have made many good friends.

Then the *New York Times, Southern Living* and *Men's Journal*

started writing articles about our cooking school. Companies like GlaxoWellcome sent some doctors to attend. Chase Manhattan Bank invited some of their most active depositors. Two former mayors of Austin (Lee Cook and Roy Butler) have also joined us at cooking school. Oops, we had been discovered.

Soon it was a squeeze to fit everyone into the restaurant's small kitchen. Also, we had a recurring nightmare that we'd show up for cooking school on Sunday morning and no one would have cleaned up from Saturday night. It never happened, thank God, but paranoia springs eternal.

When Jeff and Shanny built their new house they had their architect (Ryan Street, their oldest son) design a space for the cooking school with both indoor and outdoor kitchens. Surely there would be enough room now. Particularly if we got those bleachers. What?! Well there was this one law firm that wanted to bring all their partners—about sixty people. And then there was the time the food writers came and we had eighty people inside

on the bleachers and another thirty watching the class outside on closed-circuit television.

And so the cooking school grew and grew. Six years later we were still doing classes, and though we had plenty of recipes, there was still no cookbook. Hmm, even we can procrastinate for only so long. This cookbook is a way to welcome all of you to cooking class wherever you may be. We hope you will have as much fun as we have had. And if you're ever in Austin . . .

RESOURCES

ANTELOPE - WILD BOAR - VENISON
Broken Arrow Ranch
P.O. Box 530
Ingram, Texas 78025
www.brokenarrow.com
1-800-962-4263

RATTLESNAKE - EXOTICS - QUAIL
PHEASANT AND OTHER GAME BIRDS
Native Game
12556 WCR 1/2
Brighton, Colorado 80601
800-952-6321

GOURMET SAUCES - SMOKERS -
MANDOLINES, ETC.
Hudson's on the Bend
4304 Hudson Bend Rd.
Austin, Texas 78734
800-996-7655
www.fearlesscooking.com

CHILI PEPPERS
Los Chileros
P.O. Box 6215
Santa Fe, New Mexico 87501
505-471-6967

HERBS - SPICES
Penzey's Ltd.
P.O. Box 933
Muskeo, Wisconsin 53150-0933
414-679-7207

ALL TYPES OF WILD GAME AND BIRDS
Polaricia
P.O. Box 990204
San Francisco, California 94124
800-426-3872

GOURMET SPECIALITIES
Central Market
Austin, Texas
512-206-1000
www.centralmarket.com

INDEX